A BOOKLOVER'S
COMPANION

A BOOKLOVER'S COMPANION

Selected and Edited by

MATTHEW REISZ

London

THE FOLIO SOCIETY

2006

First published by The Folio Society in 2006
Selection © The Folio Society 2006
Text and editorial matter © Matthew Reisz 2006

Binding illustration: Cross References. Watercolour
by Jonathan Wolstenholme, 2003.
(*Private Collection / Bridgeman Art Library*)

TYPESET IN BELL AT THE FOLIO SOCIETY.
PRINTED AND BOUND BY GRAFOS S.A., BARCELONA.

CONTENTS

THE JOYS OF READING 9

BIBLIOMANIA 23

BOOKSHOPS 33

LIBRARIES 41

SENSUAL PLEASURES 53

WRITERS AND WRITING 67

CRITICS AND REVIEWS 81

DICTIONARIES 95

TRANSLATIONS 105

CENSORSHIP 119

LIFE-CHANGING BOOKS 129

READING EVERYWHERE 141

Sources and Acknowledgements 151

ILLUSTRATIONS

Woman Reading. Oil painting by Pieter Janssens Elinga,
1668–70. (*Alte Pinakothek, Munich/Artothek*)   *frontispiece*

Titus Reading. Oil painting by Rembrandt, 1656.
(*Kunsthistorisches Museum, Vienna*)   *p.* 8

The Bookworm. Oil painting by Carl Spitzweg, *c*.1850.
(*Museum Georg Schäfer/AKG Images*)   22

The Bookshop, Beijing. Oil painting by Bob Brown, 1998.
(*Private Collection/Bridgeman Art Library*)   32

A Literary Research. Oil painting by Ludwig Deutsch, 1901.
(*Private Collection/Bridgeman Art Library*)   40

A Young Woman in a Russian Hat, Holding a Book.
Oil painting by Pietro Antonio Rotari, 18th century.
(*Sotheby's Picture Library*)   52

Tolstoy Reading in the Wood. Oil painting by Ilya Repin, 1891.
(*Tretyakov State Gallery, Moscow/© 2006 Photo Scala, Florence*)   66

L'Arlésienne (*Madame Ginoux*). Oil painting by Vincent
van Gogh, 1888.
(*Metropolitan Museum of Art, New York/Lauros/Giraudon/
Bridgeman Art Library*)   80

A Lady Reading in an Interior. Oil painting by Carl Holsøe,
late 19th/early 20th century. (*Sotheby's Picture Library*)   94

Giuseppe Baretti. Oil painting by an unknown artist after
Joshua Reynolds, 1773. (*National Portrait Gallery, London*)   104

Forbidden Books (detail). Oil painting by Alexander Mark
Rossi, 1897. (*Sotheby's Picture Library*)   118

The Magdalen Reading (detail). Oil painting by Rogier
van der Weyden, before 1438. (*National Gallery, London*)   128

Chair Car. Oil painting by Edward Hopper, 1931.
(*Private Collection/Christie's Images*)   140

THE JOYS OF READING

Being young I studied for ostentation; then a little to enable
my selfe and become wiser; now for delight and recreation,
never for gaine.

Michel de Montaigne, 'Of Three Commerces' (1613)

*There are medicines that taste terrible but do us good. And there are
people who talk about books, particularly the worthier sort of 'classics', in the same way. But reading really oughtn't to be a form of
high-minded drudgery — whatever other effects it can have on our
lives, it ought first and foremost to be about* pleasure.

*It may well be, as has often been argued, that literature can
console us in our griefs, distil the wisdom of the ages, help us understand the world around us — and even make us better people. Books
can be monuments to high achievement, can call into question our
most fundamental assumptions or suggest ways we can transform
our lives. But they can also provide distraction, escapism and pleasures as straightforward and comforting as a bar of chocolate. We
are never compelled to choose between Ian Fleming and Icelandic
sagas, between Virginia Woolf and P. G. Wodehouse, or between
Dante and Damon Runyon. All can provide people — or the same
person in different moods — with many happy hours.*

*This section is devoted to the joys of reading. It brings together
some of the larger claims that have been made for the value of books,
statements of intent from major writers and some far more personal
thoughts about the intense pleasures many of us find in reading. And
it is pleasure, after all, that should always be our guide. If we ever
find ourselves turning the pages dutifully, because the text is presti-
gious or might do us good, it is surely time to stop, cut our losses —
and read something else.*

I love my books as drinkers love their wine;
The more I drink, the more they seem divine.

Francis Bennoch, 'My Books' (1878)

'Landmarks and guides in our journey through life'

Books – lighthouses erected in the sea of time.

Edwin P. Whipple (1819–86)

In reading a book which is an old favourite with me (say the first novel I ever read) I not only have the pleasure of imagination and of a critical relish of the work, but the pleasures of memory added to it. It recalls the same feelings and associations which I had in first reading it, and which I can never have again in any other way. Standard productions of this kind are links in the chain of our conscious being. They bind together the different scattered divisions of our personal identity. They are landmarks and guides in our journey through life. They are pegs and loops on which we can hang up, or from which we can take down, at pleasure, the wardrobe of a moral imagination, the relics of our best affections, the tokens and records of our happiest hours. They are 'for thoughts and for remembrance!' They are like Fortunatus's Wishing-Cap – they give us the best riches – those of Fancy; and transport us, not over half the globe, but (which is better) over half our lives, at a word's notice!

William Hazlitt, 'On Reading Old Books' (1821)

Books are the compasses and telescopes and sextants and charts which other men have prepared to help us navigate the dangerous seas of human life.

Jesse Lee Bennett, *What Books Do for You* (1923)

Diversion and consolation

While I have *Udolpho* to read, I feel as if nobody could make
me miserable.

Catherine Morland in Jane Austen's *Northanger Abbey* (1818)

I am quite transported and comforted in the midst of my
books: they give a zest to the happiest, and assuage the
anguish of the bitterest, moments of existence! Therefore,
whether distracted by the cares or the losses of my family, or
my friends, I fly to my library as the only refuge in distress:
here I learn to bear adversity with fortitude.

Pliny the Elder (AD 23–79)

> But what strange art, what magic can dispose
> The troubled mind to change its native woes?
> Or lead us willing from ourselves, to see
> Others more wretched, more undone than we?
> This, books can do; – nor this alone; they give
> New views to life, and teach us how to live;
> They soothe the grieved, the stubborn they chastise,
> Fools they admonish, and confirm the wise:
> Their aid they yield to all: they never shun
> The man of sorrow, nor the wretch undone.

George Crabbe, *The Library* (1781)

Books are for company, the best friends; in doubts counselors,
in damps comforters; Time's perspective, the home traveller's
ship, or horse, the busy man's best recreation, the opiate of
idle weariness, the mind's best ordinary, nature's garden and
seedplot of immortality.

Richard Whitlock, *Zootomia* (1654)

11

This [reading] accosteth and secondeth all my course, and every where assisteth me: It comforts me in age, and solaceth me in solitarinesse: It easeth me of the burthen of a wearysome sloth: and at all times rids me of tedious companies: it abateth the edge of fretting sorrow, on condition it be not extreme and over insolent.

Michel de Montaigne, 'Of Three Commerces' (1613)

Sir Walter Elliot, of Kellynch-Hall, in Somersetshire, was a man who, for his own amusement, never took up any book but the Baronetage; there he found occupation for an idle hour, and consolation in a distressed one . . . he could read his own history with an interest which never failed.

Opening of Jane Austen, *Persuasion* (1818)

Conferring immortality

Since honor from the honorer proceeds,
How well do they deserve, that memorize
And leave in books for all posterity
The names of worthies and their virtuous deeds;
When all their glory else, like water-weeds
Without their element, presently dies,
And all their greatness quite forgotten lies,
And when and how they flourished no man heeds.

Samuel Daniel, 'Concerning the Honor of Books' (1613)

Towers have been razed to the ground; cities have been overthrown; triumphal arches have perished from decay; nor can either pope or king find any means of more easily conferring the privilege of perpetuity than by books. The book that he has made renders its author this service in return, that so long as the book survives its author remains immortal and cannot die, as Ptolemy declares in the Prologue to the Almagest: He is not dead, he says, who has given his life to science.

The written truth of books, not transient but permanent, plainly offers itself to be observed, and by means of the pervious spherules of the eyes, passing through the vestibule of perception and the courts of imagination, enters the chamber of intellect, taking its place in the couch of memory, where it engenders the eternal truth of the mind.

Ye [books] are the golden pots in which manna is stored, and rocks flowing with honey, nay, combs of honey, most plenteous udders of the milk of life, garners ever full; ye are the tree of life and the fourfold river of Paradise, by which the human mind is nourished, and the thirsty intellect is watered and refreshed.

Richard de Bury, *Philobiblon* (1345)

In old age, the consolation of hope is reserved for the tenderness of parents, who commence a new life in their children; the faith of enthusiasts who sing hallelujahs above the clouds; and the vanity of authors who presume the immortality of their name and writings.

Close of Edward Gibbon, *Memoirs of My Life* (1796)

The voices of the wise (and lovable) dead

Live always in the best company when you read.

Sydney Smith, in *A Memoir of the Reverend Sydney Smith by his Daughter Lady Holland* (1855)

The ultimate source of pleasure derivable from all art is that it brings you into communication with the artist. What you really love in the picture or the poem is the painter or the poet whom it brings into sympathy with you across the gulf of time. He tells you what are the thoughts which some fragment of natural scenery, or some incident of human life, excited in a mind greatly wiser and more perceptive than your own. A dramatist or a novelist professes to describe different actors on his own little scene, but he is really setting forth the varying phases of his own mind. And so Dandie Dinmont, or the Antiquary, or Balfour of Burley, is merely the conductor through which [Sir Walter] Scott's personal magnetism affects our own natures. And certainly, whatever faults a critic may discover in the work, it may be said that no work in our literature places us in communication with a manlier or more lovable nature.

Leslie Stephen, 'Sir Walter Scott' (1874)

Bright books: perspectives on our weak sights,
The clear projections of discerning lights,
Burning in shining thoughts, man's posthume day,
The track of fled souls in their milkie way,
The dead alive and busy, the still voice
Of enlarged spirits, kind heaven's white decoys!
Who lives with you lives like those knowing flowers
Which in commerce with light spend all their hours;
Which shut to clouds, and shadows nicely shun,
But with glad haste unveil to kiss the sun.

Henry Vaughan, 'To His Books' (1678)

Books are ships which pass through the vast seas of time.

Francis Bacon, *Advancement of Learning* (1605)

Books are the voices of the dead. They are the main instrument of communion with the vast human procession of the other world. They are the allies of the thought of man. They are in a certain sense at enmity with the world . . . In a room well filled with them, no one has ever felt or can ever feel solitary. Second to none, as friends to the individual, they are first and foremost among the *compages*, the bonds and rivets of the race, onward from that time when they were first written on the tablets of Babylonia and Assyria, the rocks of Asia minor, and the monuments of Egypt, down to the diamond editions of Mr Pickering and Mr Frowde.

William Ewart Gladstone, *On Books and the Housing of Them* (1898)

What a blessing it is to love books as I love them, to be able to converse with the dead, and live among the unreal!

Thomas Babington Macaulay (1800–59)

Better companions than people

While you converse with lords and dukes,
I have their betters here – my books:
Fixed in an elbow-chair at ease
I choose companions as I please.
I'd rather have one single shelf
Than all my friends except yourself;
For after all that can be said
Our best acquaintance are the dead.

Dr Thomas Sheridan, 'A Letter to the Dean When in England' (1726)

People say that life is the thing, but I prefer reading.

Logan Pearsall Smith, *Afterthoughts* (1931)

The civilised pleasures – and radical impact – of the novel

I will not adopt that ungenerous and impolitic custom, so common with novel writers, of degrading, by their contemptuous censure, the very performances to the number of which they are themselves adding ... Although our productions have afforded more extensive and unaffected pleasure than those of any other literary corporation in the world, no species of composition has been so much decried ... there seems almost a general wish of decrying the capacity and undervaluing the labour of the novelist, and of slighting the performances which have only genius, wit, and taste to recommend them ... 'And what are you reading, Miss ——?' 'Oh! it is only a novel!' replies the young lady; while she lays down her book with affected indifference, or momentary shame. 'It is only *Cecilia*, or *Camilla*, or *Belinda*'; or, in short, only some work in which the greatest powers of the mind are displayed, in which the most thorough knowledge of human nature, the happiest delineations of its varieties, the liveliest effusions of wit and humour, are conveyed to the world in the best chosen language.

Jane Austen, *Northanger Abbey* (1818)

The novel has a future. It's got to have the courage to tackle new propositions without using abstractions; it's got to present us with new, really new feelings, a whole line of new emotions, which will get you out of the emotional rut. Instead of snivelling about what is or has been, or inventing new sensations in the old line, it's got to break a way through, like a hole in the wall. And the public will scream and say it is sacrilege: because, of course, when you've been jammed for a long time in a tight corner, and you really get used to its stuffiness

16

and its tightness, till you find it sufficiently cosy; then, of course, you're horrified when you see a glaring hole in what was your cosy wall. You're horrified. You back away from the cold stream of fresh air as if it were killing you. But gradually, first one and then another of the sheep filters through the gap, and finds a new world outside.

D. H. Lawrence, 'Surgery for the Novel – or a Bomb' (1923)

It appears to me quite tenable that the function of literature as a generated prize-worthy force is precisely that it does incite humanity to continued living; that it eases the mind of strain, and feeds it, I mean definitely as *nutrition of impulse.*

This idea may worry lovers of order. Just as good literature does often worry them. They regard it as dangerous, chaotic, subversive. They try every idiotic and degrading wheeze to tame it down. They try to make a bog, a marasmus, a great putridity in place of a sane and active ebullience. And they do it from sheer simian and pig-like stupidity, and from their failure to understand the function of letters.

Ezra Pound, *How to Read* (1931)

The person, be it lady or gentleman, who has not pleasure in a good novel must be intolerably stupid.

Henry Tilney in Jane Austen's *Northanger Abbey* (1818)

Epic poetry, not tragedy, the best school for virtue

To raise, and afterwards to calm the passions – to purge the soul from pride, by the examples of human miseries, which befall the greatest – in few words, to expel arrogance, and introduce compassion, are the great effects of tragedy; great, I must confess, if they were altogether as true as they are pompous. But are habits to be introduced at three hours' warning? Are radical diseases so suddenly removed? A mountebank may promise such a cure, but a skilful physician will not undertake it. An epic poem is not in so much haste: it works leisurely; the changes which it makes are slow; but the cure is likely to be more perfect. The effects of tragedy, as I said, are too violent to be lasting. If it be answered that, for this reason, tragedies are often to be seen, and the dose to be repeated, this is tacitly to confess that there is more virtue in one heroic poem than in many tragedies.

John Dryden, dedication to the *Aeneïs* (1697)

A natural aristocracy of thought

Books are the treasured wealth of the world and the fit inheritance of generations and nations. Books, the oldest and the best, stand naturally and rightfully on the shelves of every cottage. They have no cause of their own to plead, but while they enlighten and sustain the reader his common sense will not refuse them. Their authors are a natural and irresistible aristocracy in every society, and, more than kings or emperors, exert an influence on mankind.

Henry David Thoreau, *Walden* (1854)

> Here, e'en the sturdy democrat may find,
> Nor scorn their rank, the nobles of the mind;
> While kings may learn, nor blush at being shown,
> How Learning's patents abrogate their own.
> A goodly company and fair to see;
> Royal plebeians; earls of low degree;
> Beggars whose wealth enriches every clime;
> Princes who scarce can boast a mental dime;
> Crowd here together like the quaint array
> Of jostling neighbors on a market day.

John Godfrey Saxe, 'The Library' (1887)

The door to other times and places

The good book is always a book of travel; it is about life's journey.

Henry Major Tomlinson, *Out of Soundings* (1931)

> There is no Frigate like a Book
> To take us Lands away
> Nor any Coursers like a Page
> Of prancing Poetry –
> This Traverse may the poorest take
> Without oppress of Toil –
> How frugal is the Chariot
> That bears the Human Soul!

Emily Dickinson, Poem 1263 (*c.*1873)

'Bread, sweet as honey'

What position would [British] expenditure on literature take, as compared with its expenditure on luxurious eating? We talk of food for the mind, as of food for the body: now a good book contains such food inexhaustibly; it is a provision for life, and for the best part of us; yet how long most people would look at the best book before they would give the price of a turbot for it? . . . the very cheapness of literature is making even wise people forget that if a book is worth reading, it is worth buying. No book is worth anything which is not worth *much*; nor is it serviceable until it has been read, and re-read, and loved, and loved again; and marked, so that you can refer to the passages you want in it, as a soldier can seize the weapon he needs in his armoury, or a housewife bring the spice she needs from her store. Bread of flour is good; but there is bread, sweet as honey, if we would eat it, in a good book; and the family must be poor indeed, which, once in their lives, cannot, for such multipliable barley-loaves, pay their baker's bill.

John Ruskin, Sesame and Lilies (1865)

Reading is to the mind what exercise is to the body.

Joseph Addison, Tatler (1709)

I cannot live without books.

Thomas Jefferson, letter to John Adams, 10 June 1815

Seeking guidance in the works of Virgil

⌈Robert Herrick, stranded in the South Seas⌉ would study ⌈a book of Virgil's poetry⌉, as he lay with tightened belt on the floor of the old calaboose, seeking favourite passages and finding new ones only less beautiful because they lacked the consecration of remembrance. Or he would pause on random country walks; sit on the path side, gazing over the sea on the mountains of Eimeo; and dip into the *Aeneid*, seeking *sortes.* And if the oracle (as is the way of oracles) replied with no very certain nor encouraging voice, visions of England at least would throng upon the exile's memory: the busy schoolroom, the green playing-fields, holidays at home, and the perennial roar of London, and the fireside, and the white head of his father. For it is the destiny of those grave, restrained and classic writers, with whom we make enforced and often painful apprenticeship at school, to pass into the blood and become native in the memory; so that a phrase of Virgil speaks not so much of Mantua or Augustus, but of English places and the student's own irrevocable youth.

Robert Louis Stevenson, The Ebb-Tide (1894)

Readers' reward in heaven

I have sometimes dreamt, at least, that when the Day of Judgement dawns and the great conquerors and lawyers and statesmen come to receive their rewards – their crowns, their laurels, their names carved indelibly upon imperishable marble – the Almighty will turn to Peter and will say, not without a certain envy when he sees us coming with our books under our arms, 'Look, these need no reward. We have nothing to give them here. They have loved reading.'

Virginia Woolf, 'How Should One Read a Book?' (1926)

BIBLIOMANIA

What man who really loves his books delegates to any other human being, as long as there is breath in his body, the office of inducting them into their homes?

W. E. Gladstone, *On Books and the Housing of Them* (1898)

For most book-lovers, their hobby is a harmless and indeed enriching passion. We may own far more books than we are, on any reasonable estimate of our reading rate and life expectancy, ever going to get to grips with. But we tend not to have dozens of copies of the same edition of a single book. We devote a limited proportion of our waking hours to completing sets of authors we have no interest in reading. And most of the time we manage to get from one room to another without scaling walls of books or fearing that a pile may collapse on our head. Friends may think of our enthusiasm for books as a bit excessive and eccentric but hardly as a mental illness or medical condition.

Yet there is no doubt that there are people – almost but not quite exclusively men – for whom bibliomania becomes an all-consuming obsession that they will pursue across the face of the globe, sacrificing sleep, health, hygiene, work, family, leisure and all the other ordinary pleasures and duties of life. At first they may be driven by a genuine fascination with a particular author, hopes of striking it rich through finding a valuable rarity or an intense desire to outwit rival collectors, but soon it becomes an insatiable hunger as dangerous as drugs, drinking or gambling. Some go as far as to spend all the money that should have been used to feed their children; many are so preoccupied they become completely 'absent' husbands and fathers. The lucky ones are those sensible enough to reform when their wives start issuing ultimata . . .

This section is devoted to the joys of book-loving, but it also

23

includes some salutary tales, both comic and chilling, of what happens to people who step over the edge into true bibliomania – a 'disease' that can prove as hard to shake as the more obvious physical addictions . . .

The joys of bibliomania

Oh God of Gods in Zion! what a rushing river of joy gladdens my heart as often as I have a chance of going to Paris! There the days seem always short; there are the delicate collections on the fragrant book-shelves.

Richard de Bury, Philobiblon (1345)

How pure the joy, when first my hands unfold
The small, rare volume, black with tarnish'd gold!
The Eye skims restless, like the roving bee,
O'er flowers of wit, or song, or repartee,
While sweet as Springs, new-bubbling from the stone,
Glides through the breast some pleasing theme unknown.

John Ferriar, The Bibliomania: an Epistle, to Richard Heber, Esq. (1809)

He is a dark, mouldy little man, and rather dry in his manner; yet, on his favorite theme, he kindles up, and at times is even eloquent. No fox-hunter, recounting his last day's sport, could be more animated than I have seen the worthy parson, when relating his search after a curious document, which he had traced from library to library, until he fairly unearthed it in the dusty chapter-house of a cathedral. When, too, he describes some venerable manuscript, with its rich illuminations, its thick creamy vellum, its glossy ink, and the odor of the cloisters that seemed to exhale from it, he rivals the enthusiasm of a Parisian epicure, expatiating on the merits of a Perigord pie, or a *Paté de Strasbourg*.

Washington Irving, Bracebridge Hall (1822)

Rare books grow rarer every day, and often 'tis only Hope that remains at the bottom of the fourpenny boxes. Yet the Paris book-hunters cleave to the game. August is their favourite season; for in August there is least competition. Very few people are, as a rule, in Paris, and these are not tempted to loiter. The bookseller is drowsy, and glad not to have the trouble of chaffering. The English go past, and do not tarry beside a row of dusty boxes of books. The heat threatens the amateur with sunstroke. Then, says M. Octave Uzanne, in a prose *ballade* of book-hunters – then, calm, glad, heroic, the *bouquineurs* prowl forth, refreshed with hope. The brown old calf-skin wrinkles in the sun, the leaves crackle, you could poach an egg on the cover of a quarto. The dome of the Institute glitters, the sickly trees seem to wither, their leaves wax red and grey, a faint warm wind is walking the streets. Under his vast umbrella the book-hunter is secure and content; he enjoys the pleasures of the sport unvexed by poachers, and thinks less of the heat than does the deer-stalker on the bare hill-side.

Andrew Lang, *The Library* (1892)

An obsession and disease

SIR NATHANIEL: Sir, he hath never fed of the dainties that are bred in a book.

He hath not eat paper, as it were; he hath not drunk ink. His intellect is not replenished, he is only an animal, only sensible in the duller parts,

And such barren plants are set before us, that we thankful should be,

Which we of taste and feeling are, for those parts that do fructify in us more than he.

William Shakespeare, *Love's Labour's Lost*, IV.ii (*c.*1597)

A cup of coffee, eggs, and rolls
Sustain him on his morning strolls:
Unconscious of the passers-by,
He trudges on with downcast eye;
He wears a queer old hat and coat,
Suggestive of a style remote;
His manner is preoccupied, –
A shambling gait, from side to side.
For him the sleek, bright-windowed shop
Is all in vain, – he does not stop.
His thoughts are fixed on dusty shelves
Where musty volumes hide themselves.

Frank Dempster Sherman, 'The Book-Hunter' (1885)

The BIBLIOMANIA, or the collecting [of] an enormous heap of Books, without intelligent curiosity, has, since libraries have existed, been the rage with some, who would fain pass themselves on us as men of erudition. Their motley Libraries have been called the Mad-houses of the human Mind . . . The BIBLIOMANIA has never raged more violently than in the present age . . .

Bruyere has touched on this mania with humour; of such a collector (one who is fond of superb bindings only) says he, as soon as I enter his house, I am ready to faint on the stair case from a strong smell of morocco leather.

Isaac d'Israeli, Curiosities of Literature (1791)

Have not sometimes the female members of [my venerable friend Archdeacon Meadow's] household been known on occasion of some domestic emergency – or, it may be, for mere sake of keeping the lost man out of mischief – to have been searching for him on from bookstall unto bookstall, just as the mothers, wives, and daughters of other lost men hunt them through their favourite taverns or gambling-houses? Then, again, can one forget that occasion of his going to London to be examined by a committee of the House of Commons, when he suddenly disappeared with all his money in his pocket, and returned penniless, followed by a wagon containing 372 copies of rare editions of the Bible?

John Hill Burton, The Book-Hunter (1885)

It has raged chiefly in palaces, castles, halls, and gay mansions; and those things, which in general are supposed not to be inimical to health, such as cleanliness, spaciousness, and splendor, are only so many inducements towards the introduction and propagation of the BIBLIOMANIA! ... The emotions of friendship or of love are weakened or subdued as old age advances; but the influence of this passion, or rather disease, admits of no mitigation ...

[A] sober and cautious collector ... may fancy himself proof against the temptation [of booksellers' catalogues]; and will, in consequence, *call only to look at* this unique book, or set of books; but, when he views the morocco binding, silk water-tabby lining, blazing gilt edges – when he turns over the white and spotless leaves – gazes on the amplitude of margin – on a rare and lovely print introduced – and is charmed with soft and coaxing manner in which, by the skill of Herring or Mackinlay, 'leaf succeeds to leaf' – he can no longer bear up against the temptation – and confessing himself vanquished, purchases, and retreats.

The Reverend Thomas Frognall Dibdin,
The BIBLIOMANIA or Book Madness (1809)

The costs of bibliomania

The years roll back as I write, and I see myself, five-and-twenty of them ago, young, and just married . . . Many a time (my husband dining at an eating-house) did I eat only dry bread for dinner, all the while guarding and treasuring up – chiefly tied in a corner of my handkerchief for safety, fearing, if discovered, it would go in beef and mutton – a sovereign given me by a cousin, and which I destined to the purchase of 'Boswell's Life of Johnson'. I had to wait five months ere opportunity favoured me, and not until I had been some time at the Cape of Good Hope did I triumphantly carry home my volumes. But when I held them as my own in my eager hands, what were exile, and poverty, and vexation, in comparison?

'W. S.', *Spectator*, 10 December 1881

At the little shop near Portland Road Station I came upon a first edition of Gibbon, the price an absurdity – I think it was a shilling a volume . . . Having spoken with the bookseller, I walked home, took the cash, walked back again, and – carried the tomes from the west end of Euston Road to a street in Islington far beyond the *Angel*. I did it in two journeys – this being the only time in my life when I thought of Gibbon in avoirdupois. Twice – three times, reckoning the walk for the money – did I descend Euston Road and climb Pentonville on that occasion. Of the season and the weather I have no recollection; my joy in the purchase I had made drove out every other thought. Except, indeed, of the weight. I had infinite energy, but not much muscular strength, and the end of the last journey saw me upon a chair, perspiring, flaccid, aching – exultant!

George Gissing, *The Private Papers of Henry Ryecroft* (1905)

Bibliomania and family life

When I look around me and survey the persecutions to which book-lovers are subjected by their wives, I thank the goddess Fortune that she has cast my lot among the celibates; indeed, it is still one of the few serious questions I have not yet solved, viz. whether a man can at the same time be true to a wife and to bibliomania.

Eugene Field, *The Love Affairs of a Bibliomaniac* (1896)

Back from a tedious holiday
   He comes, and – Duty first – he looks
   Around for his familiar books;
But all the room's in disarray!
He searches, what's the matter, eh?
   He hunts in most unheard of nooks.
   'Were robbers here, or were they cooks,
Who seized, who stole my Books away?
Not one! What wind has blown about,
What tempest can have tossed them out,
   And cleared the shelves that used to hold them?'
No cook, no thief, no tempest came,
His lady wife, 'tis she's to blame,
   Who carted off the Books – and sold them!

F. Fertiault, 'A Domestic Event' (1888)

The room was a small one, and would in any case have only just sufficed for homely comfort, used as it evidently was for all daytime purposes; but certainly a third of the entire space was occupied by a solid mass of books, volumes stacked several rows deep against two of the walls and almost up to the ceiling . . .

'But,' I exclaimed, 'you said you only had a *few* books!

There must be five times as many here as I have.'

'I forget the exact number,' murmured Christopherson, in great agitation. 'You see, I can't arrange them properly. I have a few more in – in the other room.'

He led me across the landing, opened another door, and showed me a little bedroom. Here the encumberment was less remarkable, but one wall had completely disappeared behind volumes, and the bookishness of the air made it a disgusting thought that two persons occupied this chamber every night.

George Gissing, 'Christopherson' (1906)

> Still dumb thou sittest, with a downcast look,
> The world forgetting o'er a brown old book;
>
> While she who would be always near thee tries
> In silence to embrace thee with her eyes.
>
> Say not so sharply 'Leave me here in peace!'
> Nay! leave thy book, and from dull reading cease.

K. D. af Wirsén, 'Love and Books' (1888)

A disciplined pursuit

The purchasing done by a book collector has very little in common with that done in a bookshop by a student getting a textbook, a man of the world buying a present for his lady, or a businessman intending to while away his next train journey. I have made my most memorable purchases on trips, as a transient. Property and possession belong to the tactical sphere. Collectors are people with a tactical instinct; their experience teaches them that when they capture a strange city, the smallest antique shop can be a fortress, the most remote stationery store a key position. How many cities have revealed themselves to me in the marches I undertook in the pursuit of books!

Walter Benjamin, 'Unpacking My Library' (1931)

Illusion: 1915 [by English novelist H. M. Tomlinson] was difficult to get to. With the junk-shop owner's permission (and a shake of her head at my craziness) I crawled into and through a mass of unwashed kitchenware, dusty knick-knacks, stacks of records and soiled furniture to retrieve this untouched booklet. I felt like a fool going after it and must have looked like one as passers-by stopped to watch my contortions behind the storefront window. When I backed out of the clutter, I was covered with dirt.

David Meyer, Memoirs of a Book Snake (2001)

In his second volume of autobiography, *Ways of Escape*, Graham Greene recalled lounging in a Saigon opium den named Chez Pola in 1955. Noticing a shelf of books beside the bed and taking one down, he discovered that he'd written it. 'It was odd', he mused, 'to find two of my own novels in a *fumerie* – *Le Ministère de la Peur* and *Rocher de Brighton*. I wrote a *dédicace* in each of them.'

Reading this, most collectors of Greene probably felt, as I did, a quickening of the pulse. Imagine finding those books. Imagine *owning* them. But the thrill didn't last. This had been twenty-five years before, after all. And the big Greene collectors would already have scoured Saigon, ferreted out whatever books he left behind, and carried them back to the climate-controlled Armed Response-guarded Floridian and Bahamian bunkers that housed their treasures.

All this was assuming the story was true, and not another of the fables created by Greene for the benefit of those of us who so loyally and . . . all right, *fanatically* collected his books.

Because, make no mistake, it was personal between us and Greene.

John Baxter, A Pound of Paper (2002)

BOOKSHOPS

Many years ago I used to get my bicycle repaired occasionally at a shop run by a man who seemed to be living out some sort of Tolkeinesque fantasy. He had a long straggly beard, which made him look like a medieval wizard. Yet the strange thing was that it covered only half his face. On the other side he was completely clean-shaven.

That was certainly my most bizarre 'retail experience'. Many of the others have been in second-hand bookshops. Some, of course, are perfectly pleasant and well run, but it used to be very common to find booksellers far keener to live out some languorous Edwardian fantasy than to do anything as vulgar as actually make a sale. Classification systems and pricing policies were often equally impenetrable.

But second-hand booksellers too have a good deal to put up with. For every charmingly mischievous customer like Helene Hanff, there are several of the 'not quite certifiable lunatics' George Orwell recalled from his 'bookshop days'. This section opens with some of the most inane remarks and startling requests put to his fellow book-sellers, which Shaun Tyas assembled in his lovely collection of Book-worm Droppings. *From the customers who ask if they've got a book in stock but can't remember the author or the title (though they know it's about history and they've got a vague recollection of the colour of the cover) to those who ask to return the books they've read and murmur audibly about the outrageous price of ten pence – a bookseller's life is not always an easy one!*

'Do you have any books bound in human skin?'

'I'm very keen on human and animal interaction in Andalusia. Got anything for me?'

'Have you got anything on the history and typology of the cream bun? I'm an expert, you know.'

'I only read books about wild animals and nuns – they're so restful.'

'I need another hundred paperbacks for my new bookcase, but this time could you stick them all together, otherwise my friends take them home to read?'

'Got any books on Egypt? It's them big stone things which appeal to me. I can just imagine my kids running riot on them!'

Love poetry for spring

New York City, 8 December 1949

Savage Landor arrived safely and promptly fell open to a Roman dialogue where two cities had just been destroyed by war and everybody was being crucified and begging passing Roman soldiers to run them through and end the agony. It'll be a relief to turn to Aesop and Rhodope where all you have

34

to worry about is a famine. I do love secondhand books that open to the page some previous owner read oftenest. The day Hazlitt came he opened to 'I hate to read new books,' and I hollered 'Comrade!' to whoever owned it before me.

New York City, 25 March 1950

Frank Doel, what are you DOING over there, you are not doing ANYthing, you are just sitting AROUND.

Where is Leigh Hunt? Where is the *Oxford Verse*? Where is the Vulgate and dear goofy John Henry? I thought they'd be such nice uplifting reading for Lent and NOTHING do you send me . . .

I require a book of love poems with spring coming on. <u>No Keats or Shelley</u>, send me poets who can make love without slobbering – Wyatt or Johnson or somebody, use your own judgment. Just a nice book preferably small enough to stick in a slacks pocket and take to Central Park.

Well, don't just sit there! Go find it! i swear i don't know how that shop keeps going.

Helene Hanff corresponds with Marks & Co.,
Booksellers, at *84, Charing Cross Road* (1971)

For I bless God in the libraries of the learned and for all the booksellers in the world.

Christopher Smart, 'Jubilate Agno' (1758–63)

A reputation for 'hot books'

After the success of *Ulysses* [which she had published], writers flocked to Shakespeare and Company on the assumption that I was going to specialize in erotica . . . For instance, there was the small man with whiskers who drove up to the bookshop in a carriage – a barouche and pair hired for the occasion to impress me, as he afterwards confessed. His long arms swinging ape-like in front of him, he walked into the shop, deposited on my table a parcel that had the look of a manuscript, and introduced himself as Frank Harris ... I asked what the manuscript was about. He undid the parcel and showed me a thing called *My Life and Loves*, which he assured me went much further than Joyce. He claimed he was really the only English writer who had got 'under a woman's skin' ...

It was wicked of me, but I couldn't resist the temptation to play a little trick on Frank Harris. Once, when he was rushing to catch a train to Nice, he stopped at the bookshop for something to read on the long journey. Could I suggest something exciting? My eye wandered along the shelf where I kept a few Tauchnitz volumes. I asked him if he had read *Little Women*. He jumped at the title, which to someone with an obsession like his could have only the French meaning of *petites femmes*. He grabbed the two volumes of Louisa Alcott's 'hot book' and off he dashed to the station.

Sylvia Beach, *Shakespeare and Company* (1956)

My bookseller is a famous fisherman, as, indeed, booksellers generally are, since the methods employed by fishermen to deceive and to catch their finny prey are very similar to those employed by booksellers to attract and to entrap buyers.

Eugene Field, *The Love Affairs of a Bibliomaniac* (1896)

Books and half-smoked bloaters

'They're saying you're about to open a bookshop. That shows you're ready to chance some unlikely things' ...

'Why do you think a bookshop is unlikely?' she shouted into the wind. 'Don't people want to buy books in Hardborough?'

They've lost the wish for anything of a rarity,' said Raven, rasping away. 'There's many more kippers sold, for example, than bloaters that are half-smoked and have a more delicate flavour. Now you'll tell me, I dare say, that books oughtn't to be a rarity.'

Florence Green decides to open a bookshop in a Suffolk village,
in Penelope Fitzgerald, The Bookshop (1978)

Paranoiac customers and dead bluebottles

In a town like London there are always plenty of not quite certifiable lunatics walking the streets, and they tend to gravitate towards bookshops, because a bookshop is one of the few places where you can hang about for a long time without spending any money. In the end one gets to know these people almost at a glance. For all their big talk there is something moth-eaten and aimless about them . . .

But the real reasons I should not like to be in the book trade for life is that while I was in it I lost my love of books. A bookseller has to tell lies about books, and that gives him a distaste for them; still worse is the fact that he is constantly dusting them and hauling them to and fro . . . As soon as I went to work in the bookshop I stopped buying books. Seen in the mass, five or ten thousand at a time, books were boring and even slightly sickening. Nowadays I do buy one occasionally, but only if it is a book I want to read and can't borrow, and I never buy junk. The sweet smell of decaying paper appeals to me no longer. It is too closely associated with paranoiac customers and dead bluebottles.

George Orwell, 'Bookshop Memories' (1936)

My bookseller has dwelt so long in his corner with folios and quartos and other antique tomes that he talks in black-letter and has the modest engaging look of a brown old stout binding, and to the delectation of discriminating olefactories he exhaleth an odor of mildew and of tobacco commingled, which is more grateful to the true bibliophile than all the perfumes of Araby.

Eugene Field, *The Love Affairs of a Bibliomaniac* (1896)

'Come after the holidays'

From the outside Gottlieb's did not look promising. The building was old and decrepit, the display window so caked with dust and grime we couldn't see inside. We opened the door with trepidation, stepped over the threshold, and were immediately swallowed up by must and gloom on that beautiful spring day. Packed from floor to ceiling were tottering shelves of *sforim*, weighty religious tomes in Hebrew and Aramaic. In the maze of narrow passageways between the shelves, bare lightbulbs hung from frayed cotton cords. The air was stale. As our eyes slowly adjusted to the dark, we could make out half a dozen black-coated Hasidim with long beards and *peyes*, ritual earlocks, rocking back and forth between the stacks as they leafed through their religious texts . . .

[Upstairs], in the center of the room, were piled *thousands* of Yiddish books covered with several inches of dust, [so we told the owner] 'You have no use for the books and we do. For you they're just taking up space. We have a van parked nearby. How about if we just take them off your hands?'

I thought I saw the man waver for a moment, but he did not relent . . . he said he needed time to think it over. '*Kumt nokh yontef* . . .' he said, dismissing us with a wave of the hand. 'Come after the Jewish holidays – then we'll see.'

Aaron Lansky, *Outwitting History* (2004)

A bookseller's credo

THIS SHOP IS HAUNTED by the ghosts
Of all great literature, in hosts;
    We sell no fakes or trashes.
Lovers of books are welcome here,
No clerks will babble in your ear,
    Please smoke – but don't drop ashes!

Browse as long as you like.
Prices of all books plainly marked.
If you want to ask questions, you'll find the
    proprietor where the tobacco smoke is thickest.
We pay cash for books.
We have what you want, though you may not
    know you want it.
☛   Malnutrition of the reading faculty is a
    serious thing.
Let us prescribe for you.
             By R. & H. MIFFLIN,
                    Proprs.

Sign on the wall of the Parnassus at Home Bookshop in Brooklyn,
in Christopher Morley, *The Haunted Bookshop* (1920)

LIBRARIES

*A library can be a shelf with half a dozen books. It can even be just
an aspiration – a set of shelves waiting to be filled when its owners
can afford it. Yet, at the other end of the scale, there were fears dat-
ing back to the nineteenth century that the libraries of some private
individuals were becoming so large that the country might disap-
pear beneath the sheer weight of books. And that takes no account of
the great national and academic libraries which almost attain
Borges's unsettling ideal of containing all that has ever been – or
could ever be – thought or imagined.*

*Umberto Eco once gave a lecture on libraries in which he offered
a description of an archetypal 'bad library', without lavatories or
photocopiers, where the collection is divided up into several widely
separated catalogues, each using a different system of spellings and
abbreviations; where the subject headings are obscure and arbitrary;
where books take hours if not days to arrive from the stacks, and
then have to be returned and re-ordered every time a reader goes out
for a cup of tea. This is a (slightly) exaggerated description of many
of the great old-style academic libraries until quite recently. They
remain places of strange rituals and high ideals, full of hidden ten-
sions and passions, of dozers, daydreamers and eccentrics who seem
to spend their lives there.*

*This section celebrates many different kinds of library. Most con-
tain dozens of books, repositories of the wisdom of the ages, which*

are seldom if ever consulted. Should they be compared to 'beauties in a harem', to people ending their days in a retirement home, or perhaps to sleeping beauties waiting to be discovered and brought back to life by some future scholar?

For most people, of course, libraries have long meant either commercial circulating libraries or the neighbourhood libraries financed by local authorities that have proved so crucial to the literary and political education of working-class autodidacts. Few institutions, one might have thought, have given so much enlightenment and harmless pleasure to so many. Yet there was something about the quiet respectability of libraries that goaded the savage anarchism of Joe Orton . . .

The greatest library of them all

Those examples allowed a librarian of genius to discover the fundamental law of the Library. This philosopher observed that all books, however different from one another they might be, consist of identical elements: the space, the period, the comma, and the twenty-two letters of the alphabet. He also posited a fact which all travelers have since confirmed: *In all the Library, there are no two identical books.* From those incontrovertible premises, the librarian deduced that the Library is 'total' – perfect, complete, and whole – and that its bookshelves contain all possible combinations of the twenty-two orthographic symbols (a number which, though unimaginably vast, is not infinite) – that is, all that is able to be expressed, in every language. *All* – the detailed history of the future, the autobiographies of the archangels, the faithful catalog of the Library, thousands and thousands of false catalogs, the proof of the falsity of those false catalogs, a proof of the falsity of the *true* catalog, the gnostic gospel of Basilides, the commentary upon that gospel, the commentary

42

on the commentary on that gospel, the true story of your
death, the translation of every book into every language, the
interpolations of every book into all books, the treatise Bede
could have written (but did not) on the mythology of the
Saxon people, the lost books of Tacitus.

Jorge Luis Borges, 'The Library of Babel' (1998)

Great British libraries

Th'hast made us all thine *Heirs*: whatever we
Hereafter write, 'tis thy *Posterity*.

Henry Vaughan, 'On Thomas Bodley's Library' (1678)

Majestique Monument, and Pyramide,
Where still the shapes of parted Soules abide
Embalmed in verse! exalted soules, which now
Enjoy those Arts they woo'd soe well below!
    Which now all wonders printed plainly see,
     That have bin, are, or are to bee,
In the mysterious Librarie,
The Beatifique Bodley of the Deitie.

Abraham Cowley, 'The Book Humbly presenting it selfe
to the Universitie Librarie at *Oxford*' (1663)

The founding of a library is one of the greatest things we
can do with regard to results. It is one of the quietest of
things; but there is nothing I know of at bottom more important. Every one able to read a good book becomes a wiser
man. He becomes a similar centre of light and order and just
insight into the things around him. A collection of good
books contains all the nobleness and wisdom of the world
before us. Every heroic and victorious soul has left his stamp
upon it. A collection of books is the best of all Universities;

for the University only teaches us to read the book: you must go to the book itself for what it is. I call it a Church also – which every devout soul may enter.

Thomas Carlyle, addressing a meeting to set up
the London Library, 24 June 1840

There is, as in most libraries, a heavily charged erotic atmosphere in the Reading Room [of the London Library]: a girl undoing a button of her cardigan lifts a head from every armchair. It is hard not to imagine urgent ecstasies in the more secluded areas of Biography, but . . . the nearest I got to anything really scandalous was a report that there was a man in the French Pub in Soho who claimed to have made love to a girl among the Early Fathers. This is on the top floor and would seem to be the safest place. Frances Partridge said she thought it was very likely. 'They'd have been overexcited by all those books on theology.'

John Wells, *Rude Words* (1991)

The dubious activities of this strange old bibliophile, scholar, and crook came to light many years after he was dead. He would go to the British Museum Reading Room, ask for a particular book, and sit at one of the tables perusing it. In his mouth would be a short length of string, which he chewed and impregnated with saliva. In due course he would take this string from his mouth unobtrusively and place it into the fold of the open book before him. He would then gently close the book, put it aside and take up another for a short spell. After his saliva had done its work he would open up the first book, lightly pull away the saturated page he wanted, and secrete it upon his person. Many a time he thus made up imperfect copies in his own possession, books which either lacked a particular leaf or had wormed or defaced pages which offended him.

It is a remarkable thing that he seldom bothered to remove the tell-tale piece of string. Many, many years later, some of these copies were asked for again. They were found to be mutilated and imperfect, naturally, complete with evidence. The previous handler was always found to be Thomas J. Wise.

O. F. Snelling, *Rare Books and Rarer People* (1982)

The fog grew thicker; she [Marian Yule] looked up at the windows beneath the dome [of the British Museum Reading Room] and saw that they were a dusky yellow. Then her eye discerned an official walking along the upper gallery, and in pursuance of her grotesque humour, her mocking misery, she likened him to a black, lost soul, doomed to wander in an eternity of vain research along endless shelves. Or again, the readers who sat here at these radiating lines of desks, what were they but hapless flies caught in a huge web, its nucleus the great circle of the Catalogue? Darker, darker. From the towering wall of volumes seemed to emanate visible motes, intensifying the obscurity; in a moment the book-lined circumference of the room would be but a featureless prison-limit.

George Gissing, *New Grub Street* (1891)

Circulating libraries

SIR ANTHONY ABSOLUTE: Madam, a circulating library in a town is as an evergreen tree of diabolical knowledge! It blossoms through the year! And depend upon it, Mrs Malaprop, that they who are so fond of handling the leaves, will long for the fruit at last.

Richard Brinsley Sheridan, *The Rivals* (1775)

Think of what our Nation stands for
    Books from Boots, and country lanes,
Free speech, free passes, class distinction,
    Democracy and proper drains.

John Betjeman, 'In Westminster Abbey' (1940)

Twice, sometimes three times a week, Felicity sets out with a bundle of books under her arm, goes up in one of Andrew Brown's lifts, presents herself at the desk which is labelled 'FAB to KYT,' and smiles at the young lady who sits behind it. In Felicity's case the young lady always returns this smile, and the following dialogue then takes place: . . .

Attendant: 'Here are some of the latest, Mrs Foster.'
    [Felicity looks at the backs of these works and fails to recognise either their titles or their authors.]
Felicity (politely but disparagingly): 'I don't think I —'
Attendant (briskly): '*Prendergast's Property* — that's a very pretty story.'
Felicity (doubtfully): 'Oh . . . I never seem to like books where the people are called "Prendergast".'
Attendant: 'Well, what about *The Transept*? It's going very well, you know.'
Felicity (suspiciously): 'Is it religious?'
Attendant (surprisingly): 'Oh, no. It's about Rhodesia.'
Felicity (with conviction): 'I always hate that.'

Denis Mackail, Greenery Street (1925)

Libraries and autodidacts

We desked the small room we had set aside for our exclusive use, and did other carpentry jobbing in quite a workmanlike manner. Like newly married people who look forward to important events we made our cradle before the child was born – we shelved a corner to accommodate what we had the presumption to call a library. But we had no books, nor had we yet the means of purchasing any. I remember the late Elijah Ridings once saying to me – 'If I'd fifty pounds I'd go to Lunnon, an' buy a ton of books'; what a magnificent spectacle that presented to me!

Ben Brierley, a Lancashire weaver, setting up a mutual improvement society for his fellow workers in the 1840s, in *Home Memories* (1886)

How often I went in for warmth and a doze
The newspaper room while my world outside froze
And I took out my sardine sandwich feast.
Whitechapel Library, Aldgate East.
And the tramps and the madman and the chattering crone
The smell of their farts could turn you to stone
But anywhere, anywhere was better than home . . .

The reference library, where my thoughts were to rage.
I ate book after book, page after page.
I scoffed poetry for breakfast and novels for tea.
And plays for my supper. No more poverty.
Welcome young poet, in here you are free
to follow your star to where you should be.
That door of the library was the door into me.

And Lorca and Shelley said 'Come to the feast.'
Whitechapel Library, Aldgate East.

Bernard Kops, 'Whitechapel Library, Aldgate East' (2000)

Overwhelmed by books

His manners were less pure, but his character was equally amiable with that of his father. Twenty-two acknowledged concubines, and a library of sixty-two thousand volumes, attested the variety of his inclinations, and from the productions which he left behind him, it appears that the former as well as the latter were designed for use rather than ostentation.

Edward Gibbon on the Emperor Gordian, *The History of the Decline and Fall of the Roman Empire* (1776–88)

Lo! all in silence, all in order stand
And mighty folios first, a lordly band;
Then quartos their well-order'd ranks maintain,
And light octavos fill a spacious plain:
See yonder, ranged in more frequented rows,
A humbler band of duodecimos;
While undistinguish'd trifles swell the scene,
The last new play and fritter'd magazine.
Thus 'tis in life, where first the proud, the great,
In leagued assembly keep their cumbrous state:
Heavy and huge, they fill the world with dread,
Are much admired, and are but little read.

George Crabbe, *The Library* (1781)

The annual arrivals at the Bodleian Library are, I believe, some twenty thousand; at the British Museum, forty thousand, sheets of all kinds included. Supposing three-fourths of these to be volumes, of one size or another, and to require on average an inch of shelf space, the result will be that in every two years nearly a mile of new shelving will be required to meet the wants of a single library . . .

Nearly two-thirds, or say three-fifths, of the whole cubic

contents of a properly constructed apartment may be made a nearly solid mass of books: a vast economy which, so far as it is applied, would probably quadruple or quintuple the efficiency of our repositories as to contents, and prevent the population of Great Britain from being some centuries hence thrust into the surrounding waters by the exorbitant dimensions of their own libraries.

William Ewart Gladstone, *On Books and the Housing of Them* (1898)

The function of libraries

'What a plague do they mean,' said the little quarto ⌈in a library 'buried deep among the massive walls' of Westminster Abbey⌉, which I began to perceive was somewhat choleric, 'what a plague do they mean by keeping several thousand volumes of us shut up here, and watched by a set of old vergers like so many beauties in a harem, merely to be looked at now and then by the Dean . . . ?'

'Softly, my worthy friend,' replied I, 'you are not aware how much better you are off than most books of your generation. By being stored away in this ancient library, you are like the treasured remains of those saints and monarchs which lie enshrined in the adjoining chapels . . .'

'Sir,' said the little tome, ruffling his leaves and looking big, 'I was intended to circulate from hand to hand, like other great contemporary works; but here I have been clasped up for more than two centuries, and might have silently fallen a prey to these worms that are playing the very vengeance with my intestines, if you had not by chance given me an opportunity of uttering a last few words before I go to pieces.'

'My good friend,' rejoined I, 'very few of your contemporaries can be at present in existence; and those few owe their longevity to being immured like yourself in old libraries;

49

which, suffer me to add, instead of likening to harems, you might more properly and gratefully have compared to those infirmaries attached to religious establishments, for the benefit of the old and decrepid.'

Washington Irving, *The Sketch Book of Geoffrey Crayon* (1848)

Lest we become confused and forgetful, the function of a great library is to sort and store obscure books. This is above all the task we want libraries to perform: to hold on to books that we don't want enough to own, books of very limited appeal, unshielded by racks of Cliffs Notes or ubiquitous citations or simple notoriety. A book whose presence you crave at your bedside or whose referential or snob value you think you will need throughout life, you buy. Libraries are repositories for the out of print and the less desired, and we value them inestimably for that. The fact that most library books seldom circulate is part of the mystery and power of libraries. The books are there, waiting from age to age until their moment comes. And in the case of any given book, its moment may never come – but we have no way of predicting that, since we are unable to know now what a future time will find of interest.

Nicholson Baker, *New Yorker* (1983)

Desecrating libraries

Reading isn't an occupation we encourage among police officers. We try to keep the paper work down to a minimum.

Joe Orton, *Loot* (1967)

In a critical study of the poet, a pot-bellied old man tattooed from head to toe and clothed in only a skimpy swim-suit stood stiffly beside the name JOHN BETJEMAN ... Instead of their photograph a biography of the Lunts had tacky Christmas figurines including a stuffed snowman, red and white reindeer, and two red and white does called Jill and Judy. In Alec Clunes's biography his face was replaced by a skull with a hole in the cranium. *Glok*, an American novel by Richard G. Stern, had its author as Hedda Hopper in one of her most preposterous feathered *chapeaux*.

John Lahr, Joe Orton's biographer, describing the depredations wreaked on certain library books by him, in *Prick Up Your Ears* (1978)

SENSUAL PLEASURES

In reading, one should notice and fondle details.

Vladimir Nabokov, 'Good Readers and Good Writers' (1980)

Books provide information and entertainment, but they can also offer intense sensual pleasures. Lots of people have taken delight in the exquisite typefaces, elegant spines and musty smells of beloved old books. Others find they conjure up memories of early family life, lost schooldays or happy moments roaming in antiquarian bookshops.

This section brings together some fine descriptions of the evocative emotions people have found in books as objects, *sometimes even books in languages they were unable to read. Yet others have taken a robust contrary view, reminding us that, while elegantly balanced margins and fine woodcuts are all very well, books are meant to be* read *rather than worshipped or treasured, and that beautiful covers can often hide banal or boring writing.*

There have always been beautiful books, but the Book Beautiful refers more specifically to the products of the private press movement. This was initiated by William Morris when he set up the Kelmscott Press in 1891 as a final attempt to redeem the ugliness of late-Victorian mass production and restore the dignity of medieval craftsmanship. Many other printers followed in his footsteps, issuing even more grandiose manifestos, accepting (or rejecting) his crucial dogmas about, for example, the superiority of certain typefaces and, often after disastrous initial experimentation, slowly acquiring the skills to produce genuinely beautiful books. Their ideals are celebrated, and their pretensions mocked, in this section.

Bookish sights and smells

Pleasant to me is the glittering of the sun upon these margins, because it flickers so.

Marginal note by an Irish scribe
in a ninth-century manuscript

Of such books as I have gathered about me and made my constant companions I can truthfully say that a more delectable-flavored lot it were impossible to find. As I walk among them, touching first this one and then that, and regarding all with glances of affectionate approval, I fancy that I am walking in a splendid garden, full of charming vistas, wherein parterre after parterre of beautiful flowers is unfolded to my enraptured vision; and surely there were never other odors so delightful as the odors which my books exhale!

Eugene Field, *The Love Affairs of a Bibliomaniac* (1896)

> Dear beloved old pigskin tomes!
>   Of dingy hue – old bookish darlings!
> Oh, cluster ever round my rooms,
>   And banish strife, disputes, and snarlings.

Anon., 'Old Books' (1887)

Now, by the hearthside, I like best among books the faint perfumes of those old forgotten things that claim a little pity along with my love ... Old books of devotion, of church music, the happy and peevish fancies of religious souls, please me well. I plead guilty to liking a thing because 'tis old. I believe, were I to live two hundred years hence, I should like silk hats.

Edward Thomas, 'Recollections of November' (1902)

Conjuring up the past

I must confess that I dedicate no inconsiderable portion of my life to other people's thoughts. I dream away my life in others' speculations. I love to lose myself in other men's minds. When I am not walking, I am reading; I cannot sit and think. Books think for me . . .

How beautiful to the genuine lover of reading are the sullied leaves, and worn-out appearance, nay the very odour (beyond Russia), if we would not forget kind feelings in fastidiousness, of an old 'Circulating Library' *Tom Jones*, or *Vicar of Wakefield*. How they speak of the thousand thumbs that have turned over their pages with delight! – of some sempstress, whom they may have cheered (milliner, or harder-working mantua-maker) after her long day's needle-toil, running far into midnight, when she has snatched an hour from sleep, to stop her cares, as in some Lethean cup, in spelling out their enchanting contents! Who would have them a whit less soiled? What better condition could we desire to see them in?

Charles Lamb, 'Detached Thoughts on Books and Reading' (1833)

I know men who say they had as lief read any book in a library copy as in one from their own shelf. To me that is unintelligible. For one thing, I know every book of mine by its *scent*, and I have but to put my nose between the pages to be reminded of all sorts of things. My Gibbon, for example, my well-bound eight-volume Milman edition, which I have read and read and read again for more than thirty years – never do I open it but the scent of the noble page restores to me all the exultant happiness of that moment when I received it as a prize. Or my Shakespeare, the great Cambridge Shakespeare – it has an odour which carries me yet further back in life: for these volumes belonged to my father,

and before I was old enough to read them with understanding, it was often permitted me, as a treat, to take down one of
them from the bookcase, and reverently to turn the leaves.
The volumes smell exactly as they did in that old time, and
what a strange tenderness comes upon me when I hold one
of them in hand.

> George Gissing, *The Private Papers of Henry Ryecroft* (1905)

Books are my life, books are my love, and during the cold
months that year in Britain I stored up enough bookish living
and loving to last the rest of my life. The books I bought are
now shelved roundabout the libraries I serve, and as I pass
they call to me to hold them again in my hands. Most power-
fully does their mere sight evoke the landscapes wherein I
first encountered them, in rainy autumn, snowy winter, leafy
spring, on the fancy shelves of carpeted stores in London's
West End or in the basements of Charing Cross Road, in
seashore shops, and stalls of university and cathedral towns
in Scotland, Ireland, and England, all the sweet places of
innermost penetration and fragrant memory.

> Lawrence Clark Powell, *Books in My Baggage* (1960)

Echoes from two Russian childhoods

In the drab surroundings of this mercantile room there was a
little glass-front bookcase behind a curtain of green taffeta. It
is about that bookcase that I should like to speak now. The
bookcase of early childhood is a man's companion for life. The
arrangement of its shelves, the choice of books, the colors of
the spines are for him the color, height, and arrangement of
world literature itself. And as for books which were not
included in that first bookcase – they were never to force their
way into the universe of world literature. Every book in the

first bookcase is, willy-nilly, a classic, and not one of them can ever be expelled ...

[In orderly array] were the Germans – Schiller, Goethe, Kerner, and Shakespeare in German – in the old Leipzig and Tübingen editions, chubby little butterballs in stamped claret-colored bindings with a fine print calculated for the sharp vision of youth and with soft engravings done in a rather classical style: women with their hair down wring their hands, the lamp is always shown as an oil lamp, the horsemen have high foreheads, and the vignettes are clusters of grapes. All this was my father fighting his way as an auto-didact into the German world out of the Talmudic wilds.

Osip Mandelstam, 'The Bookcase' (1965)

The Russian Classics who had bored me at school because they were badly taught became alive and as close to me as friends. Their prose – Tolstoy's sentences, heavy as blocks of granite, Chekhov's soft as autumn leaves, Dostoyevsky's moaning and quivering like telegraph wires at night – revealed itself to me for the first time in all its beauty of lan-guage and depth and richness of meaning.

Pushkin, stale as porridge at school, cheerfully swung his strong young fist through the glass of his official portrait and stepped out of its frame, sly, daring, impudent, and smelling of snow and champagne. Lermontov, his tragic double and antithesis, leapt out of the pages of anthologies, his horse in a lather, his cloak blowing in the winds of the Caucasus and in clouds of gunsmoke.

Yevgeny Yevtushenko, *A Precocious Autobiography* (1963)

The Book Beautiful

I began printing books with the hope of producing
some which would have a definite claim to beauty,
while at the same time they should be easy to read
and should not dazzle the eye, or trouble the intellect of the reader by eccentricity of form in the
letters. I have always been a great admirer of the
calligraphy of the Middle Ages, and of the earlier
printing which took its place . . . it was the essence
of my undertaking to produce books which it
would be a pleasure to look upon as pieces of
printing and arrangement of type.

'A Note by William Morris on his Aims in
Founding the Kelmscott Press' (1891)

It was thus that in printing, and binding, Books,
not Books alone were the object of the Press
and Bindery but the creation, as by another hand
are created the flowers of the field and of the
hedgerows, of something of that Order and of that
Beauty which, on the great scale, it is the business
of life on the great scale to create; as it has been the
business of the unseen on a great scale to create the
universe. The creation of life on the great scale of
great things has been the ultimate object aimed at
by similitude in the creation of the small things
which have been the creation of the Press.

T. J. Cobden-Sanderson, a dissenting disciple of William
Morris, 'The Threefold Purpose of the Doves Press' (1908)

To the Bed of the River Thames, the river on whose banks I have printed all my printed books, I bequeath The Doves Press Fount of Type – the punches, the matrices, and the type in use at the time of my death, and may the river in its tides and flow pass over them to and from the great sea for ever and for ever, or until its tides and flow for ever cease; then may they share the fate of all the world, and pass from change to change for ever upon the Tides of Time, untouched of other use and all else.

Cobden-Sanderson, after a quarrel with his partner
Emery Walker, disposing of his beloved typeface,
Journals, 11 June 1911

The hand press printer should make his own ink, as the painter should make his own paints. Ink is not a raw material. Oil and pigments are the raw material of ink; patience in grinding is the only virtue required of the craftsman. Of patience there is this to be said. To be patient is to suffer. By their fruits men know one another, but by their suffering they are what they are. And suffering is not merely the endurance of physical or mental anguish, but of joy also.

Eric Gill, a central figure in the private press
movement (and fierce Catholic moralist),
An Essay on Typography (1931)

My greatest mistake [in his early career as a publisher] was to allow the printer to provide the paper. He produced a nasty spongy antique wove and, ignorant as I was in those days about paper and printing, I had my doubts about it from the first. I went down and helped him to print the beastly thing. I have never seen a more desperate, ludicrous – but for me at the time tragic – scene than McDermott printing *Monday or Tuesday* [by his wife and co-founder of the Press, Virginia Woolf]. He insisted upon printing the woodcuts with the letterpress. The consequence was that, in order to get the right 'colour' for the illustrations, he had to get four or five times more ink on his rollers than was right for the type. His type was soon clogged with ink; but even that was not the worst: he got so much ink on the blocks and his paper was so soft and spongy that little fluffy bits of paper were torn off with the ink and stuck to the blocks and then to the rollers and finally to the type. We had to stop every few minutes and clean everything, but even so the pages were an appalling sight.

Leonard Woolf, Beginning Again (1964),
on the early days of the Hogarth Press

If you write very obscure verse (and why shouldn't you, pray?) for which there is little or no market, you pretend that there is an enormous demand, and that the stuff has to be rationed. Only 300

copies will be printed, you say, and then the type
will be broken up for ever. Let the connoisseurs
and bibliophiles savage each other for the honour
and glory of snatching a copy. Positively no re-
print. Reproduction in whole or in part forbidden.
Three hundred copies, of which this is Number
4,312. Hand-monkeyed oklamon paper, indigo
boards in interpulped squirrel-toe, not to mention twelve point Campile Perpetua cast specially
for the occasion. Complete, unabridged, and positively unexpurgated. Thirty-five bob a knock and
a gory livid bleeding bargain at the price.

Well, I have decided to carry this thing a bit
further. I beg to announce respectfully my coming
volume of verse entitled 'Scorn for Taurus'. We
have decided to do it in eight point Caslon on
turkey-shutter paper with covers in purple cor-
duroy. But look out for the catch. When the type
has been set up, it will be instantly destroyed and
NO COPY WHATEVER WILL BE PRINTED.

Flann O'Brien, *The Best of Myles* (1968)

It is as if BOOK were an acronym for BOX OF
ORGANISED KNOWLEDGE. We have become paper-
back buyers and put up with torn spines and covers
on which telephone numbers have been ball-
pointed. We have to relearn pride in books as
objects lovely in themselves.

Anthony Burgess, writing about The Folio Society

Books to marvel at – and books to read

His Study! with what Authors is it stor'd?
In Books, not Authors, curious is my Lord;
To all their dated Backs he turns you round:
These Aldus printed, those Du Suëil has bound.
Lo, some are Vellom, and the rest as good
For all his Lordship knows, but they are Wood.
For Locke or Milton 'tis in vain to look,
These shelves admit not any modern book.

Alexander Pope, 'Epistle IV' (1731)

There is one with gold agleam,
Like the Sangreal in a dream,
Back and boards in every part
Triumph of the binder's art.
Costing more 'tis well believed,
Than the author e'er received.
But its contents? Idle tales,
Flappings of a shallop's sails!
In the treasury of learning
Scarcely worth a page's turning.

Willis Fletcher Johnson, 'My Books' (1887)

Some collectors place all their fame on the *view* of a splendid library, where volumes, arrayed in all the pomp of lettering, silk linings, triple gold bands, and tinted leather, are locked up in wire cases, and secured from the vulgar hands of the *mere reader*, dazzling our eyes like eastern beauties peering through their jalousies!

Isaac d'Israeli, *Curiosities of Literature* (1791)

They dwell in the odor of camphor,
　　They stand in a Sheraton shrine,
They are 'warranted early editions',
　　These worshipful tomes of mine; —

In their creamy 'Oxford vellum',
　　In their redolent 'crushed Levant',
With their delicate watered linings,
　　They are jewels of price, I grant; —

Blind-tooled and morocco-jointed,
　　They have Bedford's daintiest dress,
They are graceful, attenuate, polished,
　　But they gather the dust, no less.

Austin Dobson, 'My Books' (1885)

To possess few books, and those not too rich and rare for daily use, has this advantage, that the possessor can make himself master of them all, can recollect their peculiarities, and often remind himself of their contents. The man that has two or three thousand books can be familiar with them all; he that has thirty thousand can hardly have a speaking acquaintance with more than a few. The more conscientious he is, the more he becomes like Lucian's amateur, who was so much occupied in rubbing the binding of his books with sandal-wood and saffron, that he had no time left to study the contents . . .

The best of volumes may, in my estimation, be destroyed as a possession by a binding so sumptuous that no fingers dare to open it for perusal. To the feudal splendours of Mr Cobden-Sanderson, a tenpenny book in a ten-pound binding, I say fie. Perhaps the ideal library, after all, is a small one, where the books are carefully selected and thoughtfully arranged in accordance with one central code of taste, and intended to be respectfully consulted at any moment by the master of their destinies. If fortune made me possessor of one book of excessive value, I should hasten to part with it. In a little working library, to hold a first quarto of *Hamlet*, would be like entertaining a reigning monarch in a small farmhouse at harvesting.

Edmund Gosse, Introduction to *Gossip in a Library* (1891)

Sheltering among one's books

Books are companions even if you don't open them.

Benjamin Disraeli, letter to Lady Bradford, August 1878

I entrench myself in my books equally against sorrow and the weather. If the wind comes through a passage, I look about to see how I can fence it off by a better disposition of my movables; if a melancholy thought is importunate, I give another glance at my *Spenser*. When I speak of being in contact with my books, I mean it literally. I like to lean my head against them. Living in a southern climate, though in a part sufficiently northern to feel the winter, I was obliged, during that season, to take some of the books out of the study, and hang them up near the fireplace in the sitting-room, which is the only room that has such a convenience. I therefore walled myself in, in the manner above mentioned. I took a walk every day, to the astonishment of the Genoese, who used to huddle against a bit of sunny wall, like flies on a chimney-piece; but I did this only that I might so much the more enjoy my *English* evening.

Leigh Hunt, 'My Books' (1823)

In praise of reciprocal dishonesty

I do not bang or blow them about as much as I should, or oil their leather backs, or align those backs properly. They are unregimented. Only at night, when the curtains are drawn and the fire flickers, and the lights are turned off, do they come into their own and attain a collective dignity. It is very pleasant to sit with them in the firelight for a couple of minutes, not reading, not even thinking, but aware that they, with their accumulated wisdom and charm, are waiting to be used, and that my library, in its tiny imperfect way, is a successor to the great private libraries of the past. 'Do you ever lend books?' someone may say in a public-spirited tone of voice at this point. Yes, I do, and they are not returned, and still I lend books. Do I ever borrow books? I do, and I can see some of them unreturned around me. I favour reciprocal dishonesty.

E. M. Forster, 'My Library' (1951)

WRITERS AND WRITING

I first heard of him as a Greek god under a Japanese sun-
shade, reading poetry in his pyjamas, at Grantchester, – at
Grantchester upon the lawns where the river goes.

D. H. Lawrence about Rupert Brooke, in a letter
to Lady Ottoline Morrell, 30 April 1915

*Writers have always been fascinated by other writers, as mentors,
rivals, examples to emulate or avoid, and images of the kind of life
they were seeking for themselves. But although their pen portraits
are often tinged with adulation, envy or disappointment, the results
can be unforgettable. One can argue endlessly about whether
Boswell captured 'the real Dr Johnson' or whether he puts a barrier
between Johnson and us, but the personality he conjures up is as rich,
compelling and moving as almost any character in fiction. And if it
tells us as much about Boswell as about Johnson, that only adds to
its interest. The most memorable portraits are produced not by
professional biographers who clinically sift through mountains of
evidence many years later but by contemporaries with descriptive
skills and an emotional axe to grind.*

*This section brings together writers' tributes, passing comments –
often waspish – and full-scale descriptions of other writers: writers
as carefully contrived 'characters', writers debauched or almost
saintly, melancholy or overwhelmed with mirth, aggressive or col-
laborative, solitary or holding forth to admiring disciples.*

Virgil's tribute to a 'suff'ring friend'

'Love alters not for us his hard decrees,
Not tho' beneath the Thracian clime we freeze,
Or Italy's indulgent heav'n forego,
And in midwinter tread Sithonian snow;

67

Or, when the barks of elms are scorch'd, we keep
On Meroë's burning plains the Libyan sheep.
In hell, and earth, and seas, and heav'n above,
Love conquers all; and we must yield to Love.'
My Muses, here your sacred raptures end:
The verse was what I ow'd my suff'ring friend.

Virgil imagines a suitable end for the lovelorn poet Cornelius
Gallus in 'The Tenth Pastoral', translated by John Dryden (1697)

Shakespeare as apprentice butcher

Mr William Shakespeare was born at Stratford upon Avon in
the county of Warwick. His father was a butcher, and I have
been told heretofore by some of his neighbours, that when he
was a boy he exercised his father's trade, but when he killed a
calf he would do it in a high style, and make a speech.

John Aubrey, Brief Lives, late seventeenth century

Chaste courtship and drunken gaiety

[George Herbert's] visible virtues begot him much love from
a gentleman of a noble fortune; namely, Mr Charles Danvers
of Bainton, in the County of Wilts, Esq. This Mr Danvers,
having known him long, and familiarly, did so much affect
him, that he often and publicly declared a desire, that Mr Herbert would marry any of his nine daughters – for he had so
many – but rather his daughter Jane than any other, because
Jane was his beloved daughter . . .

This was a fair preparation for a marriage; but, alas! her
father died before Mr Herbert's retirement to Dauntsey: yet
some friends to both parties procured their meeting; at which
time a mutual affection entered into both their hearts, as a
conqueror enters into a surprised city; and love having got

such a possession, governed, and made there such laws and resolutions, as neither party was able to resist . . . insomuch, that she changed her name into Herbert the third day after this first interview.

This haste might in others be thought a love-frenzy, or worse; but it was not, for they had wooed so like princes, as to have select proxies; such as were true friends to both parties, such as well understood Mr Herbert's and her temper of mind, and also their estates, so well before this interview, that the suddenness was justifiable by the strictest rules of prudence; and the more, because it proved so happy to both parties.

Izaak Walton, The Life of Mr George Herbert (1670)

In a course of drunken gaiety, and gross sensuality, with intervals of study perhaps yet more criminal, with an avowed contempt of all decency and order, a total disregard of every moral, and a resolute denial of every religious obligation, he lived worthless and useless, and blazed out his youth and his health in lavish voluptuousness; till, at the age of one-and-thirty, he had exhausted the fund of life, and reduced himself to a state of weakness and decay.

Dr Johnson on the Earl of Rochester, the most obscene major
poet in the English language, Lives of the Poets, vol. 1 (1779)

Dr Johnson 'exceedingly diverted'

I have known him at times exceedingly diverted at what seemed to others a very small sport. He now laughed immoderately, without any reason that we could perceive, at our friend's making his will; called him the *testator*, and added, 'I dare say he thinks he has done a mighty thing. He won't stay till he gets home to his seat in the country, to produce this wonderful deed: he'll call up the landlord of the first inn on the road; and after a suitable preface upon mortality and the uncertainty of life, will tell him that he should not delay making his will . . .'

Mr Chambers [the friend's lawyer] did not by any means relish this jocularity and seemed impatient till he got rid of us. Johnson could not stop his merriment, but continued it all the way till he got without the Temple-gate. He then burst into such a fit of laughter, that he appeared to be almost in a convulsion; and, in order to support himself, laid hold of one of the posts at the side of the foot pavement, and sent forth peals so loud, that in the silence of the night his voice seemed to resound from Temple-bar to Fleet-ditch.

James Boswell, The Life of Samuel Johnson (1791)

You have but two topics, yourself and me, and I'm sick of both.

Dr Samuel Johnson, quoted in Boswell, London Journal, 9 May 1763

Boswell in love – as told in an index

Lewis, Mrs (Louisa), actress. JB to call Louisa in journal, 84; receives JB, 85; JB visits, 88; JB's increased feeling for, 89; JB discusses love with, 94–5; JB anticipates delight with, 96; JB lends two guineas to, 97; disregards opinion of world, 97–8; discusses religion with JB, 101; JB entreats to be kind, 101; uneasiness of discourages JB, 104; JB declares passion for, 107; promises to make JB blessed, 107; JB sees every day, 109; JB talks with freely of love connections, 112; JB promises to support child, should one be born, 113; makes assignation with JB, 116; consummation with JB interrupted, 117; promises to pass night with JB, 118; JB likes better and better, 121; JB's felicity delayed, 126; to stay with JB Wednesday night, 130; agrees to go to Hayward's with JB, 135; account of her birth, unhappy marriage, and separation, 135; spends night with JB at Hayward's, 137–40; JB has tea with, 141–2; JB afraid of a rival, 144; JB feels coolness for, 145; reads French with JB, 145; JB resolves to keep affection for alive, 149; JB incredulous at infection from, 155–6; JB enraged at perfidy of, 158; JB discusses infection with and takes leave of, 158–61; JB asks his two guineas back, 174–5; returns JB's guineas, 187; mentioned, 12, 98, 116.

A typical example of James Boswell's tangled relations with
women, as summarised in the Index to Frederick A. Pottle's
edition of his *London Journal* (1950)

Coleridge – 'a very lachrymose and morbid gentleman'

Another occasional visitor . . . was Mr Flosky, a very lachry-mose and morbid gentleman, of some note in the literary world, but in his own estimation of much more merit than name. The part of his character which recommended him to Mr Glowry was his very fine sense of the grim and the tear-ful. No one could relate a dismal story with so many minutiae of supererogatory wretchedness. No one could call up *a raw-head and bloody-bones* with so many adjuncts and circum-stances of ghastliness. Mystery was his mental element. He lived in the midst of that visionary world in which nothing is but what is not. He dreamed with his eyes open, and saw ghosts dancing round him at noontide. He had been in his youth an enthusiast for liberty, and had hailed the dawn of the French Revolution as the promise of a day that was to banish war and slavery, and every form of vice and misery, from the face of the earth. Because all this was not done, he deduced that nothing was done; and from this deduction, according to his system of logic, he drew a conclusion that worse than nothing was done; that the overthrow of the feudal fortresses

of tyranny and superstition was the greatest calamity that
had ever befallen mankind.

Thomas Love Peacock mocks Coleridge in the character
of Mr Flosky, in *Nightmare Abbey* (1818)

Wordsworth 'either mad or inspired'

Mr Wordsworth, in his person, is above the middle size, with
marked features, and an air somewhat stately and Quixotic.
He reminds one of some of Holbein's heads, grave, saturnine,
with a slight indication of sly humour, kept under by the manners of the age or by the pretensions of the person. He has a
peculiar sweetness in his smile, and great depth and manli-
ness and a rugged harmony, in the tones of his voice. His
manner of reading his own poetry is particularly imposing;
and in his favourite passages his eye beams with preternatural
lustre, and the meaning labours slowly up from his swelling
breast. No one who has seen him at these moments could go
away with an impression that he was a 'man of no mark or
likelihood'. Perhaps the comment of his face is necessary to
convey a full idea of his poetry. His language may not be intelligible, but his manner is not to be mistaken. It is clear that he
is either mad or inspired.

William Hazlitt, 'Mr Wordsworth' (1825)

Takin' his family out in a string and niver geeing the dreari-
est bit of notice to 'em; standin' by hisself and stoppin' behind
agapin', with his jaws workin' the whoal time; but niver no
crackin' wi' 'em, nor no pleasure in 'em – a desolate-minded
man, ye kna' – it was poetry as did it.

A local innkeeper describing William Wordsworth,
quoted in *Still More Christmas Crackers* (2000)

Shelley picks a fight at dinner

I went a little after the time, and seated myself in the place kept for me at the table, right opposite Shelley himself, as I was told after, for I did not then know what hectic, spare, weakly yet intellectual-looking creature it was carving a bit of broccoli or cabbage in his plate, as if it had been the substantial wing of a chicken . . .

In a few minutes Shelley opened the conversation by saying in the most feminine and gentle voice, 'As to that detestable religion, the Christian –' I looked astounded, but, casting a glance round the table, easily saw by ——'s expression of ecstasy and the women's simper, I was to be set at that evening *vi et armis*. No reply, however, was made to this sally during dinner, but when the dessert came, and the servant was gone, to it we went like fiends. —— and —— were deists. I felt exactly like a stag at bay, and resolved to gore without mercy.

The Autobiography and Memoirs of Benjamin
Robert Haydon, 1786–1846 (1927)

He always was, and is, a kind of ghastly object: colourless, pallid, tuneless, without health or warmth or vigour; the sound of him shrieky, frosty, as if a ghost were trying to 'sing' to us.

Thomas Carlyle on Shelley, *Reminiscences* (1881)

William Morris and his 'dark silent medieval woman'

He [William Morris] designs with his own head and hands all the figures and patterns used in his glass and tapestry and furthermore works the latter, stitch by stitch with his own fingers – aided by those of his wife and little girls. Ah, *ma chère*, such a wife! *J'en reviens pas* – she haunts me still. A figure cut out of a missal – out of one of Rossetti's or Hunt's pictures – to say this gives but a faint idea of her, because when such an image puts on flesh and blood, it is an apparition of fearful and wonderful intensity. It's hard to say [whether] she's a grand synthesis of all the pre-Raphaelite pictures ever made – or they a 'keen analysis' of her – whether she's an original or a copy ... After dinner Morris read us one of his unpublished poems, from the second series of un-'Earthly Paradise', and his wife having a bad toothache, lay on the sofa, with her handkerchief to her face. There was something very quaint and remote from our actual life, it seemed to me, in the whole scene: Morris reading in his flowing antique numbers a legend of prodigies and terrors (the story of Bellerophon, it was), around us all the picturesque bric-à-brac of the apartment (every article of furniture literally a 'specimen' of something or other), and in the corner this dark silent medieval woman with her medieval toothache.

Henry James, letter to his sister Alice James, 12 March 1869

Chesterton in his element

Best is it to see him in his favourite habitat of Bohemian Soho. There in certain obscure yet excellent French restaurants, with Hilaire Belloc and other writers and talkers, he may be seen, sitting behind a tall tankard of lager or a flagon of Chianti, eternally unravelling the mysterious tangle of living ideas; now rising mountainously on his feet to overshadow the company with weighty argument, anon brandishing a wine-bottle as he insists upon defending some controversial point until 'we break the furniture'; and always chuckling at his own wit and the sallies of others, as he fights the battle of ideas with indefatigable and unconquerable good-humour.

Holbrook Jackson, 'G. K. Chesterton' (1908)

His Chesterton is no more authentic and much less amusing than the mythical figure of twenty years ago, the roaring, beer-swilling swashbuckler at whose name capitalists and cocoa-drinkers turned pale.

Hugh Kingsmill reviewing a book by Hugh Kenner (1948)

Huxley's encyclopaedic conversation

You could always tell by his conversation which volume of the *Encyclopaedia Britannica* he'd been reading. One day it would be Alps, Andes and Apennines, and the next it would be the Himalayas and the Hippocratic Oath.

Bertrand Russell on Aldous Huxley,
letter to R. W. Clark, July 1965

Coping with editors, publishers and readers

Editor: A person employed on a newspaper, whose business it is to separate the wheat from the chaff, and to see that the chaff gets printed.

Elbert Hubbard, *The Roycroft Dictionary* (1914)

'It is for you', said [Mr Longman], 'to think whether our names on your title page are not worth more to you than the increased payment.' This seemed to me to savour of that high-flown doctrine of the contempt of money which I have never admired. I did think much of Messrs Longman's name, but I liked it best at the bottom of a cheque.

Anthony Trollope negotiates with his publisher,
in *An Autobiography* (1883)

[Dryden] has often said to me in confidence, that the world would never suspect him to be so great a poet, if he had not assured them so frequently in his prefaces that it was impossible they could either doubt or forget it.

Jonathan Swift, *A Tale of a Tub* (1704)

Writers as heroes and writers as humbugs

The Hero as *Man of Letters* . . . has hardly lasted above a century in the world yet. Never, till about a hundred years ago, was there seen any figure of a Great Soul living apart in that anomalous manner; endeavouring to speak forth the inspiration that was in him by Printed Books, and find place and subsistence by what the world would please to give him for doing that. Much had been sold and bought, and left to make its own bargain in the marketplace; but the inspired wisdom of a Heroic Soul never till then, in that naked manner. He, with his copy-rights and copy-wrongs, in his squalid garret, in his rusty coat; ruling (for this is what he does), from his grave, after death, whole nations and generations who would, or would not, give him bread while living – is a rather curious spectacle! Few shapes of Heroism can be more unexpected.

Thomas Carlyle, *On Heroes, Hero-Worship and the Heroic in History* (1841)

When a gentleman is cudgelling his brain to find any rhyme for sorrow, besides borrow and to-morrow, his woes are nearer at an end than he thinks for.

'That's the way of poets,' said Warrington. 'They fall in love, jilt, or are jilted; they suffer and cry out that they suffer more than any other mortals; and when they have experienced feelings enough they note them down in a book, and take the book to market. All poets are humbugs; directly a man begins to sell his feelings for money he's a humbug. If a poet gets a pain in his side from too good a dinner, he bellows "Ai, Ai," louder than Prometheus.'

William Makepeace Thackeray,
The History of Pendennis (1848–50)

I can never get people to understand that poetry is the expression of *excited passion*, and that there is no such thing as a life of passion any more than a continuous earthquake or an eternal fever. Besides, who would ever *shave* themselves in such a state?

Lord Byron, letter to Thomas Moore, 5 July 1821

The art of writing, like the art of love, runs all the way from a kind of routine hard to distinguish from piling bricks to a kind of frenzy closely related to delirium tremens.

H. L. Mencken, *Minority Report* (1956)

Elegy, *n*. A composition in verse, in which, without employing any of the methods of humor, the writer aims to produce in the reader's mind the dampest kind of dejection. The most famous example in English begins somewhat like this:

> The cur foretells the knell of parting day;
>   The loafing herd winds slowly o'er the lea
> The wise man homeward plods; I only stay
>   To fiddle-faddle in a minor key.

Ambrose Bierce,
The Devil's Dictionary (1911)

Fond farewells

Yet once more, O ye laurels, and once more
Ye myrtles brown, with ivy never sere,
I come to pluck your berries harsh and crude,
And with forced fingers rude,
Shatter your leaves before the mellowing year.
Bitter constraint, and sad occasion dear,
Compels me to disturb your season due:
For Lycidas is dead, dead ere his prime
Young Lycidas, and hath not left his peer:
Who would not sing for Lycidas? He knew
Himself to sing, and build the lofty rhyme.
He must not float upon his watery bier
Unwept, and welter to the parching wind,
Without the meed of some melodious tear.

Milton laments the death of fellow poet
Edward King in *Lycidas* (1637)

He has outsoared the shadow of our night;
Envy and calumny and hate and pain,
And that unrest which men miscall delight,
Can touch him not and torture not again;
From the contagion of the world's slow stain
He is secure, and now can never mourn
A heart grown cold, a head grown gray in vain;
Nor, when the spirit's self has ceased to burn,
With sparkless ashes load an unlamented urn.

Shelley pays tribute to John Keats in
Adonais, XL (1821)

They told me, Heraclitus, they told me you were dead,
They brought me bitter news to hear and bitter tears to shed.
I wept as I remember'd how often you and I
Had tired the sun with talking and sent him down the sky.

And now that thou art lying, my dear old Carian guest,
A handful of grey ashes, long, long ago at rest,
Still are thy pleasant voices, thy nightingales, awake;
For Death, he taketh all away, but them he cannot take.

Callimachus remembers his friend 'Heraclitus',
translated by William Cory (1845)

CRITICS AND REVIEWS

Professor Phelps's *Happiness* is second only to a rubber duck as the ideal bathtub companion.

Dorothy Parker, *New Yorker* (1927)

There are writers who forget their children's birthdays, even their children's names, but none ever forgets a bad review. Some can still recite them verbatim decades later. A few sensitive souls are said to have wasted away and died in response to fierce reviews. Others have immediately hit back — it was thus that Byron launched his poetic career — or pursued lifelong vendettas.

Some literary critics have claimed that theirs is a noble calling, a crucial tool for spreading the humanising influence of great literature. But what about daily or weekly newspaper reviewing? It has often been attacked as lazy and irresponsible, a racket tainted by back-scratching and score-settling. Most authors take a pretty dim view of it, claiming that reviewers are often more interested in being witty or bitchy at their expense than in offering informed assessments of their work. Yet many poets, novelists and playwrights have themselves proved highly effective in savaging their competitors.

Really skilful hatchet jobs can, of course, make entertaining reading. But much of the most interesting criticism is produced by creative writers looking to ensure the best reception for their books. Many have tried to define the terms by which they hope to be judged or, in attacking others, have set out their own literary values. And, when all else fails, few have been squeamish about roping in friends to review their books . . .

Pope defines the perfect critic

A perfect Judge will *read* each Work of Wit
With the same Spirit that its Author *writ*,
Survey the *Whole*, nor seek slight Faults to find,
Where *Nature moves*, and *Rapture warms* the Mind;
Nor lose, for that malignant dull Delight,
The *gen'rous Pleasure* to be *charm'd* with Wit.
But in such Lays as neither *ebb*, nor *flow*,
Correctly cold, and *regularly low*,
That shunning Faults, one quiet *Tenour* keep;
We cannot *blame* indeed – but we can *sleep*.

Alexander Pope, *An Essay on Criticism* (1711)

Critic, *n.* A person who boasts himself hard to please because
nobody tries to please him.

There is a land of pure delight,
Beyond the Jordan's flood,
Where saints, appareled all in white,
Fling back the critic's mud.

Ambrose Bierce, *The Devil's Dictionary* (1911)

To sum up my whole Charge against this Author [Pope] in a
few Words: He has ridiculed both the present Ministry and
the last; abused great Statesmen and great Generals; nay the
Treaties of whole Nations have not escaped him, nor has the
Royal Dignity it self been omitted in the Progress of his
Satyr; and all this he has done just at the Meeting of a new
Parliament. I hope a proper Authority may be made use of to
bring him to condign Punishment: In the mean while I doubt
not, if the Persons most concern'd would but order Mr
Bernard Lintott, the Printer and Publisher of this dangerous

Piece, to be taken into Custody, and examin'd; many further Discoveries might be made both of this Poet's and his Abetter's secret Designs, which are doubtless of the utmost Importance to the Government.

'Esdras Barnivelt, Apothecary' – a pseudonym for Pope himself –
savages Alexander Pope's *Rape of the Lock*, in *A Key to the Lock* (1715)

They can scarce be called critics who must hear and read a thing before they will venture to declare their opinion. Anybody can do that.

John Gay (1685–1732)

The English critic – all mouth: when he opens it his head disappears.

Frank Harris (1856–1931)

Decorous gardens and Shakespearian forests

Shakespeare was the theatre's greatest craftsman. He wasted no tortured ratiocination on his plays. Instead he filled them with the gaudy heroes that all of us see ourselves becoming on some bright tomorrow, and the lowly frauds and clowns we are today.

H. L. Mencken (1880–1956)

The work of a correct and regular writer is a garden accurately formed and diligently planted, varied with shades, and scented with flowers; the composition of *Shakespeare* is a forest, in which oaks extend their branches, and pines tower in the air, interspersed sometimes with weeds and brambles, and sometimes giving shelter to myrtles and to roses; filling the eye with awful pomp, and gratifying the mind with endless diversity. Other poets display cabinets of precious rarities, minutely finished, wrought into shape, and polished unto brightness. *Shakespeare* opens a mine which contains gold and diamonds in inexhaustible plenty, though clouded by incrustations, debased by impurities, and mingled with a mass of meaner minerals.

Dr Samuel Johnson, *Preface to Shakespeare* (1765)

That the *Lives [of the Poets]* continue to be read, admired, and edited, is in itself a high proof of the eminence of Johnson's intellect; because, as serious criticism, they can hardly appear to the modern reader to be very far removed from the futile. Johnson's aesthetic judgments are almost invariably subtle, or solid, or bold; they have always some good quality to recommend them – except one: they are never right. That is an unfortunate deficiency; but no one can doubt that Johnson has made up for it, and that his wit has saved all. He has managed to be wrong so cleverly, that nobody minds.

Lytton Strachey, 'The Lives of the Poets' (1906)

All that is bad in Shakespeare's works is bad elaborately and of malice aforethought.

Lord Macaulay, 'John Dryden' (1828)

Not a single one [of Shakespeare's sonnets] is very admirable ... They are hot and pothery: there is much condensation, little delicacy; like raspberry jam without cream, without crust, without bread.

Walter Savage Landor, 'Southey and Landor',
Imaginary Conversations (1848)

Byron confronts his critics

Is it true, what Shelley writes me, that poor John Keats died at Rome of the *Quarterly Review*? I am very sorry for it, though I think he took the wrong line as a poet, and was spoilt by Cockneyfying, and Suburbing, and versifying Tooke's Pantheon and Lempriere's Dictionary. I know, by experience, that a savage review is Hemlock to a sucking author; and the one on me (which produced the *English Bards, etc.*) knocked me down – but I got up again. Instead of bursting a blood-vessel, I drank three bottles of Claret, and began an answer, finding that there was nothing in the Article for which I could lawfully knock Jeffrey on the head, in an honourable way. However, I would not be the person who wrote the homicidal article, for all the honour and glory in the World, though I by no means approve of that School of Scribbling which it treats upon.

Lord Byron, letter to John Murray, 26 April 1821

Such is the force of wit! But not belong
To me the arrows of satiric song;
The royal vices of our age demand
A keener weapon, and a mightier hand.
Still there are follies, e'en for me to chase,
And yield at least amusement in the race;
Laugh when I laugh, I seek no other fame;
The cry is up, and scribblers are my game.
Speed, Pegasus! – ye strains of great and small,
Ode, epic, elegy, have at you all!

Lord Byron, *English Bards and Scotch Reviewers* (1809)

The poetic death of a beautiful woman

I had now gone so far as the conception of a Raven – the bird of ill omen – monotonously repeating the one word, 'Nevermore,' at the conclusion of each stanza, in a poem of melancholy tone, and in length about one hundred lines. Now, never losing sight of the object *supremeness*, or perfection, at all points, I asked myself – 'Of all melancholy topics, what, according to the *universal* understanding of mankind, is the *most* melancholy?' Death – was the obvious reply. 'And when', I asked, 'is this most melancholy of topics most poetical?' . . . the answer, here also, is obvious – 'When it most closely allies itself to *Beauty*: the death, then, of a beautiful woman is, unquestionably, the most poetical topic in the world – and equally is it beyond doubt that the lips best suited for such topic are those of a bereaved lover.'

Edgar Allan Poe explains how he produced 'The Raven',
in 'The Philosophy of Composition' (1846)

The triumph of the book reviewer

We are surprised at first sight, that writers should wish to comment on one another; it appears a tedious mode of stating opinions, and a needless confusion of personal facts with abstract arguments; and some, especially authors who have been censured, say that the cause is laziness – that it is easier to write a review than a book – and that reviewers are, as Coleridge declared, a species of maggots, inferior to book-worms, living on the delicious brains of real genius . . .

In truth, review-writing but exemplifies the casual character of modern literature. Everything about it is temporary and fragmentary. Look at a railway stall; you see books of every colour – blue, yellow, crimson, 'ring-streaked, speckled, and spotted', on every subject, in every style, of every opinion, with every conceivable difference, celestial or sublunary, maleficent, beneficent – but all small. People take their literature in morsels, as they take sandwiches on a journey. The volumes at least, as you see clearly, are not meant to be everlasting. It may be all very well for a pure essence like poetry to be immortal in a perishable world; it has no feeling; but paper cannot endure it, paste cannot bear it, string has no heart for it.

Walter Bagehot, 'The First Edinburgh Reviewers' (1855)

The struggle for existence among books is nowadays as severe as among men. If a writer has friends connected with the press, it is the plain duty of those friends to do their utmost to help him. What matters if they exaggerate, or even lie? The simple, sober truth has no chance whatever of being listened to, and it's only by volume of shouting that the ear of the public is held.

Jasper Milvain, the archetypal 'literary man of 1882', explains the reviewing racket, in George Gissing, *New Grub Street* (1891)

'How can a man like Macready', Dickens demanded, 'fret and fume and chafe himself for such lice of literature as these' – the 'lice' are writers in Sunday newspapers – 'rotten creatures with men's forms and devils' hearts?' Yet lice as they are, when they 'discharge their pigmy arrows' even Dickens with all his genius and his magnificent vitality cannot help but mind and has to make a vow to overcome his rage and 'to gain the victory by being indifferent and bidding them whistle on' . . .

Tennyson and Dickens are both angry and hurt; they are also ashamed of themselves for feeling such emotions. The reviewer was a louse; his bite was contemptible; yet his bite was painful. His bite injured vanity; it injured reputation; it injured sales. Undoubtedly in the nineteenth century the reviewer was a formidable insect; he had considerable power over the author's sensibility; and upon the public taste. He could hurt the author; he could persuade the public either to buy or to refrain from buying.

Virginia Woolf, 'Reviewing' (1939)

87

Reviewing as fish scraping and sausage selling

I know, quite intimately, at least five men who review novels (if I may say so respectfully) in the bulk; as men scrape fish in a fish shop . . .

I have an immense admiration – more than an intense admiration, a bewildered and sudden admiration – for [them]. I cannot do it, because there has been put into my mind either by my Creator or by some little Daemon, a sort of catch which jabs up and stops me reading after the first two or three lines. Indeed, when I do read a book (alas for me!) it is nearly always because I open it at random in the middle and find something that strikes me. But the beginning always knocks me out. When I read a beginning like this: 'It was already dark and she was waiting,' my mind gives way and I go back to some of the more simple problems of arithmetic or to a cross-word puzzle.

Hilaire Belloc, 'On Not Reading Books' (1929)

What would he [Charles Lamb] have to say of the novels, for example? These commodities are all very well in their way, no doubt. But let us have no illusions as to what their way is. The poulterer who sells strings of sausages does not pretend that every individual sausage is itself remarkable. He does not assure us that 'this is a sausage that gives furiously to think', or 'this is a singularly beautiful and human sausage', or 'this is undoubtedly the sausage of the year'. Why are such distinctions drawn by the publisher? When he publishes, as he sometimes does, a novel that is a book (or at any rate would be a book if it were decently bound) then by all means let him proclaim its difference – even at the risk of scaring away the majority of readers.

Max Beerbohm, 'Books within Books' (1920)

Every critic is in the position, so to speak, of God, and has no responsibility save to whatever may be visible of his own decency. He can smite without being smitten. He challenges other men's work, and is exposed to no comparable challenge of his own. The more reputations he breaks, the more his own reputation is secured – and there is no lawful agency to determine, as he himself professes to determine in the case of other men, whether his motives are honest and his methods are fair. Jahweh Himself is less irresponsible, for he must at least keep the respect of the theologians, or go down to ruin with His predecessors.

H. L. Mencken, *Minority Report* (1956)

George Eliot on 'silly novels'

The real drama of Evangelicalism – and it has abundance of fine drama for any one who has genius enough to discern and reproduce it – lies among the middle and the lower classes; and are not evangelical opinions understood to give an especial interest in the weak things of the earth, rather than in the mighty? Why, then, cannot our Evangelical lady novelists show us the operation of their religious views among people (there really are many such in the world) who keep no carriage, 'not so much as a brass-bound gig', who even manage to eat their dinner without a silver fork, and in whose mouths the authoress's questionable English would be strictly consistent? Why can we not have pictures of religious life among the industrial classes in England, as interesting as Mrs Stowe's pictures of religious life among the negroes? Instead of this, pious ladies nauseate us with novels which remind us of what we sometimes see in a worldly woman recently 'converted'; she is as fond of a fine dinner table as before, but she invites clergymen instead of beaux; she thinks as much of her

89

dress as before, but she adopts a more sober choice of colours and patterns; her conversation is as trivial as before, but the triviality is flavoured with Gospel instead of gossip.

George Eliot, 'Silly Novels by Lady Novelists' (1856)

The book *is* interesting – only I wish the characters would talk a little less like the heroes and heroines of police reports.

George Eliot on *Jane Eyre*, letter to Charles Bray, 11 June 1848

Dwelling on excellence and 'the true poetic accent'

It is because criticism has so little kept in the pure intellectual sphere, has so little detached itself from practice, has been so directly polemical and controversial, that it has ill accomplished, in this country, its best spiritual work; which is to keep man from a self-satisfaction which is retarding and vulgarising, to lead him towards perfection, by making his mind dwell upon what is excellent in itself, and the absolute beauty and fitness of things . . .

But then comes another question as to the subject-matter which literary criticism should most seek. Here, in general, its course is determined for it by the idea which is the law of its being; the idea of a disinterested endeavour to learn and propagate the best that is known and thought in the world, and thus to establish a current of fresh and true ideas.

Matthew Arnold, 'The Function of Criticism at the Present Time' (1865)

Meaning is of the intellect, poetry is not. If it were, the eighteenth century would have been able to write it better. As matters actually stand, who are the English poets of that age in whom pre-eminently one can hear and recognise the true poetic accent emerging clearly from the contemporary dialect? These four: Collins, Christopher Smart, Cowper, and

Blake. And what other characteristic had these four in common? They were mad.

A. E. Housman, *The Name and Nature of Poetry* (1933)

Moccasins and broken twigs

In his little box of stage properties he kept six or eight cunning devices, tricks, artifices, for his savages and woodsmen to deceive and circumvent each other with, and he was never so happy as when he was working these innocent things and seeing them go. A favorite one was to make a moccasined person tread in the tracks of the moccasined enemy, and thus hide his own trail. Cooper wore out barrels and barrels of moccasins in working that trick. Another stage-property that he pulled out of his box pretty frequently was his broken twig. He prized his broken twig above all the rest of his effects, and worked it the hardest. It is a restful chapter in any book of his when somebody doesn't step on a dry twig and alarm all the reds and whites for two hundred yards around. Every time a Cooper person is in peril, and absolute silence is worth four dollars a minute, he is sure to step on a dry twig.

Mark Twain, 'Fenimore Cooper's Literary Offences' (1897)

Austen on Scott and Scott on Austen

Walter Scott has no business to write novels, especially good ones. – It is not fair. – He has Fame & Profit enough as a Poet, and should not be taking the bread out of other people's mouths. – I do not like him, & do not mean to like Waverley if I can help it – but fear I must . . . I have made up my mind to like no Novels really, but Miss Edgeworth's, Yours & my own.

Jane Austen, letter to her niece, aspiring novelist
Anna Austen, 28 September 1814

91

That young lady has a talent for describing the involvements and feelings and characters of ordinary life, which is to me the most wonderful I have ever met with. The big Bow-Wow strain I can do myself like any now going; but the exquisite touch which renders ordinary common-place things and characters interesting from the truth of the description and the sentiment is denied to me.

Diary of Sir Walter Scott, 12 March 1826

Definitive Dismissals

The covers of this book are too far apart.

Review attributed to Ambrose Bierce (1842–*c.*1914)

I can't read [Ben] Jonson, especially his comedies. To me he appears to move in a wide sea of glue.

Lord Tennyson, in Hallam Tennyson,
Alfred Lord Tennyson (1897)

The whole of [*Paradise Lost*] is such barbarous trash, so outrageously offensive to reason and to common sense that one is naturally led to wonder how it can have been tolerated by a people, among whom astronomy, navigation, and chemistry are understood.

William Cobbett, *Year's Residence,
in the United States of America* (1818)

Most of his writings exhibit the sluttish magnificence of a Russian noble, all vermin diamonds, dirty linen and inestimable sables.

Lord Macaulay, 'John Dryden' (1828)

He writes the worst English that I have ever encountered. It reminds me of a string of wet sponges; it reminds me of tattered washing on the line; it reminds me of stale bean soup, of college yells, of dogs barking idiotically through endless nights. It is so bad that a sort of grandeur creeps into it. It drags itself out of a dark abysm . . . of pish, and crawls insanely up the topmost pinnacle of posh. It is rumble and bumble. It is flap and doodle. It is balder and dash.

H. L. Mencken on President Warren G. Harding,
On Politics (1956)

What a clumsy *olla putrida* James Joyce is! Nothing but old fags and cabbage-stumps of quotations from the Bible and the rest, stewed in the juice of deliberate, journalistic dirty-mindedness.

D. H. Lawrence, letter to Aldous Huxley, 15 August 1928

Of all the morbid trash I ever saw, that beat everything. I thought of writing him a letter, advising a couple of anti-bilious pills before bedtime for a few weeks.

Old John Yule assesses a novel called *The Optimist*,
in George Gissing, *New Grub Street* (1891)

DICTIONARIES

Dictionary, *n.* A malevolent literary device for cramping the growth of a language and making it hard and inelastic. This dictionary, however, is a most useful work.

Ambrose Bierce, *The Devil's Dictionary* (1911)

Everyone knows that dictionaries are useful tools, and very convenient, since (as a particularly uninspired copywriter once put it) they tend to be 'alphabetised for easy reference'. Yet there have always been fierce debates about their methods and underlying purpose. Can they hope to capture the essence of a language or never do more than offer a momentary snapshot of a constantly changing picture? Should they describe *how people actually use words or* prescribe *how they ought to? (And how far is the notion of 'good usage' merely a form of pedantic snobbery?)*

Dictionary-makers face dilemmas about the right balance between definitions (even of the simplest words, which can only be pinned down by using more obscure ones) and citations. Dictionaries that grandly ignore obscenities, jargon and the latest street slang risk seeming stuffy; those that try to include them can seem ephemeral, or out of date even on publication. There are many stories about people eagerly searching dictionaries for four-letter words and then being outraged when they found them – or when they didn't.

Many of these topics are already debated in the Preface to Dr Johnson's splendidly vigorous, learned and opinionated Dictionary of the English Language *(1755). This is not only a great literary monument but a book with a strange afterlife as the leading authority on the English language at the time of the American Constitution – still sometimes consulted when there are legal arguments about what exactly the Founding Fathers meant by 'declaring war' or other such phrases.*

Dictionaries have always played a role in national self-definition. They have been required to establish and police distinctions between English and American usage. And they have been recruited into wider struggles between Britain and the leading nations of Continental Europe. Major dictionaries are inevitably a tribute to a country's philology and scholarly enterprise. But many of them also make strong implicit claims about the superiority of national languages and 'national character' . . .

Forget foreign fashions!

Let Gallants therefore skip no more from hence
To Italie, France, Spaine, and with expence
Waste time and faire estates, to learne new fashions
Of complimentall phrases, soft temptations
To glorious beggary: Here let them hand
This Booke; here studie, reade, and understand:
Then shall they find varietie at Home,
As curious as at Paris, or at Rome.

John Ford congratulating Henry Cockeram,
author of the first *English Dictionarie* (1623)

Bizarre digressions and 'creatures well known'

The best work of this period [before Dr Johnson's great *Dictionary*] was the *Universal Etymological Dictionary* compiled by Nathan Bailey, a schoolmaster from Stepney. First published in 1721, Bailey's dictionary went through thirty editions over the next eighty-one years. It was more useful and wide-ranging than its predecessors, but its definitions were often poor: 'cat' was 'a creature well known', 'to get' was defined simply as 'to obtain', 'cool' meant 'cooling or cold', 'black' was 'a colour', 'strawberry' 'a well known fruit', and 'to wash' meant 'to cleanse by washing' (although 'washing' was not defined). It was also full of bizarre digressions, red herrings and cack-handed attempts to explain popular sayings.

Henry Hitchings, Dr Johnson's Dictionary (2005)

The limitations of lexicography

Those who have been persuaded to think well of my design, require that it should fix our language, and put a stop to those alterations which time and chance have hitherto been suffered to make in it without opposition. With this consequence I will confess that I flattered myself for a while; but now begin to fear that I have indulged expectation which neither reason nor experience can justify. When we see men grow old and die at a certain time one after another, from century to century, we laugh at the elixir that promises to prolong life to a thousand years; and with equal justice may the lexicographer be derided, who being able to produce no example of a nation that has preserved their words and phrases from mutability, shall imagine that his dictionary can embalm the language, and secure it from corruption and decay, that it is in his power to change sublunary nature, or clear the world at once from folly, vanity, and affectation.

With this hope, however, academies have been instituted, to guard the avenues of the language, to retain fugitives, and repulse intruders; but their vigilance and activity have hitherto been vain; sounds are too volatile and subtile for legal restraints; to enchain syllable, and to lash the wind, are equally the undertakings of pride, unwilling to measure its desires by its strength.

Dr Samuel Johnson, Preface to the
Dictionary of the English Language (1755)

A Johnsonian ABC

AMBERGRIS. A fragrant drug, that melts almost like wax, commonly of a greyish or ash colour, used both as a perfume and a cordial. It is found on the sea coasts of several warm countries, and on the western coasts of Ireland. Some imagine it to be the excrement of a bird, which, being melted by the heat of the sun, and washed off the shore by the waves, is swallowed by whales, who return it back in the condition we find it. Others conclude it to be the excrement of a cetaceous fish, because sometimes found in the intestines of such animals. But we have no instance of any excrement capable of melting like wax; and if it were the excrement of a whale, it should rather be found where these animals abound, as about Greenland.

BACKBITER. A privy calumniator; a censurer of the absent.

COTQUEEN. A man who busies himself with women's affairs.

X is a letter, which, though found in Saxon words, begins no word in the English language.

YUX. The hiccough.

ZOOTOMIST. A dissector of the bodies of brute beasts.

Dr Samuel Johnson, sample definitions from the
Dictionary of the English Language (1755)

Lexicographical Gems

Bible-puncher; black coat; crow; cushion-smiter; devil-dodger; haul-devil; holy Joe; pulpit-thumper; sky-pilot.

> Synonyms for 'clergyman' listed in Joseph Marks, *Harrap's French–English Dictionary of Slang and Colloquialisms* (1970)

Black. White. Light red. Day. Intensely black.

> Definition of a single word, pronounced *jawn*, in J. G. Hava's *Arabic–English Dictionary* (1964)

carphology. Delirious fumbling with the bedclothes, &c.

> *Shorter Oxford English Dictionary* (2002)

Cooie, Cooey, n. a peculiar whistling sound used by the Australian aborigines and bushmen as a call or signal.

> *The British Universities Modern English Illustrated Dictionary* (1924)

Little miracles of discriminatory precision are contained in the distinctions between such simpletons as a *nebekh*, a *shlemiel*, a *shmendrick*, a *shnook*; or between such dolts as a *klutz*, a *yold*, a *Kuni Lemmel*, a *shlep*, a *Chaim Yankel*. All of them inhabit the kingdom of the ineffectual, but each is assigned a separate place in the roll call.

> Leo Rosten, *The New Joys of Yiddish* (2003)

Trying to find love with a bilingual dictionary

About the year 1794, a German, recently imported into Bristol, had happened to hear of Mrs X, a wealthy widow. He thought it would be a good speculation to offer himself to the lady's notice as well qualified to 'succeed' to the late Mr X; and accordingly waited on the lady with that intention. Having no great familiarity with English, he provided himself with a copy of one of the dictionaries I have mentioned; and, on being announced to the lady, he determined to open his proposal with this introductory sentence – Madam, having heard that Mr X, late your husband, is dead: but coming to the last word 'gestorben' (dead), he was at a loss for the English equivalent; so, hastily pulling out his dictionary (a large 8vo.), he turned to the word 'sterben' (to die), and there found – but what he found will be best collected from the dialogue which followed, as reported by the lady:

German. Madam, hahfing heard that Mein Herr X, late your man, is . . . is, dat is – has – *kicked de bucket.*

Thomas De Quincey, 'Anglo-German Dictionaries' (1823)

Dictionaries and national identity

A Dictionary is an historical monument, the history of a nation contemplated from one point of view, and the wrong ways into which a language has wandered, or attempted to wander, may be nearly as instructive as the right ones in which it has travelled: as much may be learned, or nearly as much, from its failures as its successes, from its follies as from its wisdom.

Richard Chenevix Trench, *On Some Deficiencies in Our English Dictionaries* (1857)

A capital advantage of this reform in these States would be that it would make a difference between the English orthography and the American. This will startle those who have not attended to the subject; but I am confident that such an event is an object of vast political consequence. The alteration, however small, would encourage the publication of books in our own country. It would render it, in some measure, necessary that all books should be printed in America . . .

Besides this, a national language is a band of national unity. Every engine should be employed to render the people of this country national; to call their attachments home to their own country; and to inspire them with a pride of national character. However they may boast of Independence and the freedom of their government, yet their opinions are not sufficiently independent; an astonishing respect for the arts and literature of their parent country, and a blind imitation of its manners . . . turns their attention from their own interests, and prevents their respecting themselves.

Noah Webster, *Dissertations on the English Language* (1789)

God and the Oxford English Dictionary

I think it [his appointment as Editor of *The New English Dictionary*, which became the *OED*] was God's will. In times of faith, I am sure of it. I look back & see that every step of my life has been as it were imposed upon me – not a thing of choice; and that the whole training of my life with its multitudinous & irregular incursions into nearly every science & many arts, seems to have had the express purpose of fitting me to do this Dictionary . . . So I work on with a firm belief (at most times) that I am doing what God has fitted me for, & so made my duty; & a hope that He will strengthen me to see the end of it . . . But I am only an instrument, only the means that He has provided, & there is no credit due to me, except that of trying to do my duty.

Sir James A. H. Murray, letter to Lord Bryce, 15 December 1903

The structure now reared will have to be added to, continued, and extended with time, but it will remain, it is believed, the greatest body of fact upon which all future work will be built. It is never possible to forecast the needs and notions of those who come after us, but with our present knowledge it is not easy to conceive which new feature can now be added to English lexicography.

Sir James A. H. Murray, *The Evolution of English Lexicography* (1900)

A passion for dictionaries

My curiosity rapidly grew into a passion. I was soon unable to go near a second-hand bookshop or library without seeking out the shelves where the foreign language dictionaries were kept. I would scour books in friends' houses with a similar need to 'pan for gold'. My collection of wonderful words with no equivalents in the English language grew even longer, and I started to make a shortlist of my favourites: **nakhur**, for example, is a Persian word (which may not even be known to most native speakers) meaning 'a camel that won't give milk until her nostrils have been tickled'; and **areojarekput**, the Inuit for 'to exchange wives for a few days only'. Many describe strange or unbelievable things. When and why, for example, would a man be described as a **mirilopotes**, Ancient Greek for 'a gulper of coaldust'? And could the Japanese samurai really have used the verb **tsuji-giri**, meaning 'to try out a new sword on a passer-by'?

Adam Jacot de Boinod, *The Meaning of Tingo* (2005)

Webster's Dictionary, Whitaker's Almanack, and Bradshaw's Railway Guide should be sufficient for any ordinary library; it will be time enough to go beyond these when the mass of useful and entertaining matter which they provide has been mastered.

Samuel Butler, 'Ramblings in Cheapside' (1890)

TRANSLATIONS

And now I have him made so well acquainted with our toong
As that he may in English verse as in his owne bee soong.

Arthur Golding, Preface to his translation
of Ovid's *Metamorphoses* (1567)

*Translation of literature or other serious writing is a famously
impossible task. The Authorised Version of the Bible has shaped
English sensibility ever since 1611, not least by domesticating a lot
of hitherto alien Hebrew idioms and expressions, yet Hebrew speakers tend to find it painfully inadequate if not actively repellent.
Germans may claim that the celebrated Tieck-Schlegel version of
Shakespeare is better than the Bard himself; Baudelaire may have
found poetic gold in Edgar Allen Poe's creaky doggerel. But much is
inevitably 'lost in translation'.*

*Great translations can exert a huge influence on national litera-
tures. Shakespeare's style was shaped by Golding's Ovid; his Roman
plays derive from North's Plutarch. Pope's Homer and Dryden's
Virgil define a heroic style in English verse just as surely as their
'mock heroics' underlie subsequent satiric modes. Pope's 'Imitations
of Horace', Dr Johnson's recreations of Juvenal, FitzGerald's
Omar Khayyám and Vikram Seth's verse novel in the style of Pushkin are all landmarks.*

*Yet major writers translating or reworking other major writers
face many of the same problems as translators of bawdy epigrams or
pulp fiction. All have to make decisions about whether Roman generals or Japanese geishas should sound intriguingly alien or just like
modern Britons; whether always to translate a word by the same
word; and how to deal with jokes, word play, topical references and
sporting metaphors. Should a witty character be given any genuinely amusing remark or one close to the original which just isn't*

funny in English? Should criminals speak a kind of generalised low-life slang or a more specific argot which will soon seem very dated? The bad news is that no translation will ever satisfy everybody. The good news is that the job requires such linguistic sensitivity and attention to detail that computers will never replace humans.

Ancient troubles with women

A woman is a maddening creature
and gives pleasure twice at most,
once when she gives up her virtue
once when she gives up the ghost.

Robin Skelton's version of a much translated
epigram by Palladas (1971)

Graecinus (well I wot) thou told'st me once
I could not be in love with two at once.
By thee deceived, by thee surprised am I,
For now I love two women equally.
Both are well favoured, both rich in array,
Which is the loveliest it is hard to say.
This seems the fairest, so doth that to me,
And this doth please me most, and so doth she.
Even as a boat tossed by contrary wind,
So with this love and that, wavers my mind.
Venus, why doublest thou my endless smart?
Was not one wench enough to grieve my heart?
Why add'st thou stars to heaven, leaves to green woods,
And to the vast deep sea fresh water floods?

Ovid, *Amores*, II.10, translated by Christopher Marlowe (*c.*1600)

'I doubt if all be gay within the house'

ERIPHYLA (*within*): O, I am smitten with a hatchet's jaw;
    And that in deed and not in word alone.
CHORUS: I thought I heard a sound within the house
    Unlike the voice of one that leaps for joy.
ERIPHYLA: He splits my skull, not in a friendly way,
    Once more: he purposes to kill me dead.
CHORUS: I would not be reputed rash, but yet
    I doubt if all be gay within the house.
ERIPHYLA: O! O! another stroke! that makes the third.
    He stabs me to the heart against my wish.
CHORUS: If that be so, thy state of health is poor;
    But thine arithmetic is quite correct.

A. E. Housman, a leading classical scholar, parodying the style of late-Victorian translation in 'Fragment of a Greek Tragedy' (1883)

A composite Horatian ode

Say what slim youth, with moist perfumes
    Bedaub'd, now courts thy fond embrace,
There, where the frequent rose-tree blooms,
    And makes the grot so sweet a place?
Pyrrha, for whom with such an air
Do you bind back your golden hair?

Oft, alas! shall he deplore
    Vows unkept by thee;
Oft, the Gods he would adore
    Frowning he shall see;
Oft astonished, see the main
All afoam with wind and rain,

Who now, all credulous, all gay,
    Enjoys thy smile, on whose vain pride
    Thy fickle favour shines untry'd,
And soft deceitful breezes play.

For Me, the sacred Tablet shows
That I have hung my dripping Cloaths
At Neptune's Shrine: And now on Shore
Secure, I'll tempt the Deep no more.

Horace's Ode to Pyrrha (i.5) in a composite version with stanzas taken
from four different translations by Christopher Smart (1722–71);
Patrick Branwell Brontë (1817–48); William Boscawen
(1752–1811); and William Duncombe (1690–1769)

Thaw follows frost; hard on the heel of spring
    Treads summer sure to die, for hard on hers
Comes autumn, with his apples scattering;
    Then back to wintertide, when nothing stirs.

From A. E. Housman's version of Horace, *Odes* iv.7, which he once
described as 'the most beautiful poem in ancient literature' (1897)

Making the Bible accessible

This threatening and forbidding the lay people to read the
scriptures is not for the love of your souls (which they care for
as the fox doth for the geese) is evident and clearer than the
sun, inasmuch as they permit and suffer you to read Robin
Hood and Bevis of Hampton, Hercules, Hector and Troilus
with a thousand histories and fables of love and wantonness
and of ribaldry as filthy as heart can think, to corrupt the
minds of you withal, clean contrary to the doctrine of Christ
and of his apostles ... Now saying they permit you freely to
read those things which corrupt your minds and rob you of

the kingdom of God and Christ and bring the wrath of God upon you how is this forbidding for the love of your souls?

William Tyndale, *The Obedience of a Christian Man* (1528)

Happy is the man that delighted in the Scripture, and thrice happy that meditateth in it day and night.

But how shall men meditate in that, which they cannot understand? ...

Translation it is that openeth the window, to let in the light; that breaketh the shell, that we may eat the kernel; that putteth aside the curtain, that we may look into the most Holy place; that removeth the cover of the well, that we may come by the water; even as Jacob rolled away the stone from the mouth of the well, by which means the flocks of Laban were watered. Indeed without translation into the vulgar tongue, the unlearned are but like children at Jacob's well (which is deep) without a bucket or something to draw with ...

'Translators to the Reader', in the Authorised Version of the Bible (1611)

That prudent Mother, while She admired the beauties of the sacred writings, was convinced that, unrestricted, no reading more improper could be permitted a young Woman. Many of the narratives can only tend to excite ideas the worst calculated for a female breast: Every thing is called plainly and roundly by its name; and the annals of a Brothel would scarcely furnish a greater choice of indecent expressions. Yet this is the Book which young Women are recommended to study; which is put into the hands of Children, able to comprehend little more than those passages of which they had better remain ignorant; and which but too frequently inculcates the first rudiments of vice, and gives the first alarm to the still sleeping passions.

Matthew Lewis, *The Monk* (1796)

Dressing another man's vineyard

Slaves we are, and labour on another man's plantation; we dress the vineyard, but the wine is the owner's: if the soil be sometimes barren, then we are sure of being scourged: if it be fruitful, and our care succeeds, we are not thanked; for the proud reader will only say, the poor drudge has done his duty. But this is nothing to what follows; for, being obliged to make his sense intelligible, we are forced to untune our own verses, that we may give his meaning to the reader. He, who invents, is master of his thoughts and words: he can turn and vary them as he pleases, till he renders them harmonious; but the wretched translator has no such privilege: for, being tied to the thoughts, he must make what music he can in the expression; and, for that reason, it cannot always be so sweet as that of the original . . .

Lay by Virgil, I beseech your Lordship, and all my better sort of judges, when you take up my version; and it will appear a passable beauty when the original Muse is absent. But, like Spenser's false Florimel made of snow, it melts and vanishes when the true one comes in sight.

John Dryden, dedication to the Aeneïs (1697)

Keeping alive the spirit of Homer

That which in my Opinion ought to be the Endeavour of any one who translates *Homer* is above all things to keep alive that Spirit and Fire which makes his chief Character . . . with whatever Judgment and Study a Man may proceed, or with whatever Happiness he may perform such a Work; he must hope to please but a few, those only who have at once a Taste of Poetry, and competent Learning. For to satisfy such as want either, is not in the Nature of this Undertaking; since a

meer Modern Wit can like nothing that is not *Modern*, and a
Pedant nothing that is not *Greek*.

Alexander Pope, Preface to his translation of the *Iliad* (1715)

It is a pretty poem, Mr Pope, but you must not call it Homer.

Classical scholar Richard Bentley on Pope's Homer,
quoted in Johnson's *Lives of the Poets* (1791)

Thy mighty Scholiast, whose unwearied pains
Made Horace dull, and humbled Milton's strains.
Turn what they will to Verse, their toil is vain,
Critics like me shall make it Prose again.

Pope returns the compliment and savages Bentley's
pedantry, *Dunciad*, Book IV (1743)

Much have I travelled in the realms of gold,
    And many goodly states and kingdoms seen;
    Round many western islands have I been
Which bards in fealty to Apollo hold.
Oft of one wide expanse had I been told
    That deep-browed Homer ruled as his desmesne;
    Yet never did I breathe its pure serene
Till I heard Chapman speak out loud and bold:
Then felt I like some watcher of the skies
    When a new planet swims into his ken;
Or like stout Cortez when with eagle eyes
    He stared at the Pacific – and all his men
Look'd at each with a wild surmise –
    Silent, upon a peak in Darien.

John Keats, 'On First Looking into
Chapman's Homer' (1816)

As eminently as Homer is plain, so eminently is the Elizabethan literature in general, and Chapman in particular, fanciful. Steeped in humour and fantasticality up to its very lips, the Elizabethan age, newly arrived at the free use of the human faculties after their long term of bondage, and delighting to exercise them freely, suffers from its own extravagance in this first exercise of them, can hardly bring itself to see an object quietly or to describe it temperately. Happily, in the translation of the Bible, the sacred character of their original inspired the translators with such respect that they did not dare to give the rein to their own fancies in dealing with it. But, in dealing with works of profane literature, in dealing with poetical works above all, which highly stimulated them, one may say that the minds of the Elizabethan translators were *too* active; that they could not forbear importing so much of their own, and this of a most peculiar and Elizabethan character, into their original, that they effaced the character of the original itself.

Matthew Arnold, *On Translating Homer* (1861)

From translation to original

My father was a scholar and knew Greek.
When I was five years old, I asked him once
'What do you read about?' 'The siege of Troy.'
'What is a siege and what is Troy?' Whereat
He piled up chairs and tables for a town,
Set me a-top for Priam, called our cat
– Helen, enticed away from home (he said)
By wicked Paris, who couched somewhere close
Under the footstool . . .

112

It happened, two or three years afterward,
That – I and playmates playing at Troy's Siege –
My father came upon our make-believe.
'How would you like to read yourself the tale
Properly told, of which I gave you first
Merely such notion as a boy could bear?
Pope, now, would give you the precise account
Of what, some day, by dint of scholarship,
You'll hear – who knows? – from Homer's very mouth.'

Robert Browning, 'Development' (1889)

At will I breathe the classic air,
The wanderings of Ulysses share;
Or see the plume of Bayard flow
Among my books.

Samuel Minturn Peck, 'Among my Books' (1886)

A tragic novel as comic ballad

Werther had a love for Charlotte
    Such as words could never utter;
Would you know how first he met her?
    She was cutting bread and butter.

Charlotte was a married lady,
    And a moral man was Werther,
And, for all the wealth of Indies,
    Would do nothing for to hurt her.

So he sighed and pined and ogled.
    And his passion boiled and bubbled,
Till he blew his silly brains out,
    And no more by it was troubled.

113

Charlotte, having seen his body
  Borne before her on a shutter,
Like a well-conducted person,
  Went on cutting bread and butter.

William Makepeace Thackeray, 'Sorrows of Werther',
rewriting Goethe's *Sorrows of Young Werther* (1855)

Villon the Victorian

Suppose you screeve? or go cheap-jack?
  Or fake the broads? or fig a nag?
Or thimble-rig? or knap a yack?
  Or pitch a snide? or smash a rag?
  Suppose you duff? or nose and lag?
Or get the straight, and land your pot?
  How do you melt the multy swag?
Booze and the blowens cop the lot.

William Ernest Henley's version of François Villon's fifteenth-century
'*Ballade de bonne doctrine*' (1908), using Victorian underworld slang

Où est ce Tipperary?

C'est à Tip, Tip, à Tipperary
Où nous allons, mes amis,
Et c'est chic, chic, à Tipperary
Mais mon dieu, c'est loin d'ici –
Où est ce Tipperary?
J'm'en fous, et toi aussi,
Mais c'est pour Tip, Tip, Tip, pour Tipperary
Que nous quittons Paris!

French translation of 'It's a Long Way to Tipperary',
quoted in *Still More Christmas Crackers* (2000)

Communicating with phrase books

> My cousin is deaf,
> Kindly bring me a hatchet,
> Pray pass me the pepper,
> What pretty cretonne,
> What time is the train?
> It is late,
> It is early,
> It's running on schedule,
> It's here,
> It has gone.
> I've written six letters,
> I've written no letters,
> Pray fetch me a horse,
> I have need of a groom,
> This isn't my passport,
> This isn't my hatbox,
> Please show me the way
> To Napoleon's tomb.
>
> Song by Noël Coward from the musical *Sail Away*,
> consisting of 'useless useful phrases' commonly
> listed for tourists abroad (1961)

Lost in translation

Intelligent men of no scholarship, on reading Horace, Theocritus, and other poets, through the medium of translation, have often wondered how those writers obtained their glory. And they well might. The translation is no more like the original, than a walking-stick is like a flowering bough.

Leigh Hunt, 'A Word on Translation from the Poets' (1833)

115

The extreme difficulty of translation, its extreme subtlety, its artistic quality, is seen also in this: that the great prose effects which have vitally moved one civilisation are nearly always unknown to another; and this is not only through the imperfection of language, but through the sheer impossibility of rendering the full effect of the original, save by some piece of luck or some stroke of genius. An example is Rousseau's *Social Contract.* Of the very few scholarly men who have dealt with the subject of the French Revolution in England, not one understands why Rousseau's *Social Contract* had its enormous effect. As certainly no Frenchman I ever met had the least conception of the effect the Book of Common Prayer has upon an English reader.

Hilaire Belloc, 'On Translation' (1929)

Invisible, insane.

Translation offered by a computer for the phrase
'Out of sight, out of mind'

What may very probably be the most complex type of event yet produced in the evolution of the cosmos.

I. A. Richards on the translation of Chinese
philosophical texts into English (1953)

Capturing Russian smells and idioms

Without in any way seeming incorrect or awkward, the English prose in the translation I had read nonetheless exuded a 'strange' or 'alien' flavor, which gave me much pleasure – something like the pleasure of arriving in a foreign city and smelling its unfamiliar odors for the first time. Although the English was not awkward in any sense, it felt almost as if many idioms had been translated quite literally, rather than replaced by cultural equivalents. This allowed me to vicariously feel what it might be like to speak and hear Russian, to use Russian idioms, to smell Russian smells, and so on. Perhaps it was simply the fact that the translator was from England whereas I was from America that gave the book a slightly 'alien' flavor, but whatever the reason, that flavor was there, and I savored it. Perhaps deludedly, perhaps not, I felt as if I had genuinely read a Russian novel, had genuinely experienced Dostoyevsky, all through the medium of English.

Douglas Hofstadter, Le Ton beau de Marot (1997)

The translator's dilemma

When one has done one's best, and is sure that that best is better than so many will take pains to do, though far from the best that *might be done*, one likes to make an end of the matter by Print. I suppose very few People have ever taken such Pains in Translation as I have: though certainly not to be literal. But at all Costs, a Thing must *live*: with a transfusion of one's own worse Life if one can't retain the Original's better. Better a live Sparrow than a stuffed Eagle.

Edward Fitzgerald, translator of Omar Khayyám,
letter to Edward Cowell, 27 April 1859

CENSORSHIP

Our civilisation cannot afford to let the censor-moron loose.

D. H. Lawrence, letter to Morris Ernst, 10 November 1928

It is a sign of the power of words that those in authority have always tried to prevent certain books being printed. Dictators such as Stalin, willing and able to send millions to their deaths, quaked before the power of lyric poetry. While they have obviously targeted works that overtly criticised or mocked them, tyrants have often been equally fierce towards writings that don't mention them at all but just open up alternative ways of thinking and feeling. Yet no one, as the enemies of censorship have often pointed out, has a monopoly on truth. It is only those convinced of their own infallibility or who brook no rivals to their dogmas that try and shut others up.

Censorship remains controversial and politically sensitive. Few believe in absolute freedom of speech, and the lines that should be drawn to exclude blasphemy, pornography, 'revisionist' history, racial or religious abuse are constantly being argued over. Yet there are surely several good reasons why lovers of books and literature should tend to be very wary of censorship. Some of the greatest writers in English have had their works mutilated by the red pencil of the prude or the philistine. Several have hit back with eloquent treatises in favour of freedom of expression – and the rights of other people to say things we find idiotic, upsetting or even offensive. Yet the best case against censorship surely comes from looking at what *has been censored in the past. The Bible and Shakespeare were cleaned up; 'lewd passages' removed from classical texts (or parked in an appendix, as if for the convenience of dirty-minded schoolboys); Victorian adults were protected from 'facts of life' ten-year-olds can now discover on television every day. In 1924 the Lord Chamberlain objected to the word 'hips' when a dress was described as 'slimming*

119

over the hips'. 'Ye Gods' had to replace 'Jesus' as an expletive in a play performed in 1961. The line 'I've strained meself' was removed from another. (Novels often fared even worse, with whole paragraphs or sections sliced out.) Would anyone seriously claim today that the British public needed such protection?

The case for free speech

> This is true Liberty, when free-born men
> Having to advise the public may speak free,
> Which he who can, and will, deserv's high praise
> Who neither can nor will may hold his peace;
> What can be juster in a State than this?
>
> Euripides, *Suppliant Women* (quoted at the
> head of Milton's *Areopagitica*, 1644)

And indeed we see it ever falleth out that the forbidden writing is thought to be certain sparks of a truth that fly up in the faces of those that seek to choke it, and tread it out, whereas a book authorized is thought to be but *temporis voces*, the language of the time.

> Francis Bacon, *An Advertisement Touching the
> Controversies of the Church of England* (1589–91)

Books are not absolutely dead things, but doe contain a potencie of life in them to be as active as that soule was whose progeny they are; nay they do preserve as in a violl the purest efficacie and extraction of that living intellect that bred them. I know they are as lively, and as vigorously productive, as those fabulous Dragons teeth; and being sown up and down, may chance to spring up armed men. And yet on the other hand unlesse warinesse be us'd, as good almost kill a Man as kill a good Book; who kills a Man kills a reasonable creature,

Gods Image; but hee who destroyes a good Booke, kills reason it selfe, kills the Image of God, as it were in the eye. Many a man lives a burden to the Earth; but a good Booke is the pretious life-blood of a master spirit, imbalm'd and treasur'd up on purpose to a life beyond life . . . We should be wary therefore what persecution we raise against the living labours of publick men, how we spill that season'd life of man preserv'd and stor'd up in Books; since we see a kinde of homicide may be thus committed, sometimes a martyrdome, and if it extend to the whole impression, a kinde of massacre, whereof the execution ends not in the slaying of an elementall life, but strikes at that ethereall and fift essence, the breath of reason it selfe, slaies an immortality rather then a life.

John Milton, 'Areopagitica', addressed to
'the Parliament of England' (1644)

By means of books we communicate to friends as well as foes what we cannot safely entrust to messengers; since the book is generally allowed access to the chambers of princes, from which the voice of its author would be rigidly excluded, as Tertullian observes at the beginning of his *Apologeticus.* When shut up in prison and in bonds, and utterly deprived of bodily liberty, we use books as ambassadors to our friends, and entrust them with the conduct of our cause, and send them where to go ourselves would incur the penalty of death.

Richard de Bury, *Philobiblon* (1345)

Many most able persons . . . regard the discipline of education as a precedent for persecution. They say, 'I would no sooner let the nation at large read that bad book than I would let my children read it.' They refuse to admit that the age of the children makes any difference. At heart they think that they are wiser than the mass of mankind, just as they are wiser than

their children, and would regulate the studies of both unhesi-
tatingly. But experience shows that no man is on all points so
wise as the mass of men after a good discussion ... And the
worst is, that the minds of the would-be persecutors are themselves unfixed: their opinions are in a perpetual flux; they
would persecute all others for tenets which yesterday they had
not heard of and which they will not believe tomorrow.

Walter Bagehot, 'The Metaphysical Basis of Tolerance' (1874)

The right to cause offence

Toleration or liberty have no sense or use except as toleration
of opinions that are considered damnable, and liberty to do
what seems wrong.

George Bernard Shaw, Preface to
The Shewing-up of Blanco Posnet (1911)

Hence arises the particular unhappiness of that business,
which other callings are no way liable to; they who follow
printing being scarce able to do anything in their way of getting a living, which shall not probably give offence to some,
and perhaps to many; whereas the smith, the shoemaker, the
carpenter, or the man of any other trade, may work indiffer-
ently for people of all persuasions, without offending any of
them; and the merchant may buy and sell with Jews, Turks,
heretics and infidels of all sorts, and get money by every one
of them, without giving offence to the most orthodox, of any
sort; or suffering the least censure or ill-will on the account
from any man whatever ...

If all printers were determined not to print anything till
they were sure it would offend nobody, there would be very
little printed.

Benjamin Franklin, 'An Apology for Printers' (1731)

It is not the feeling sure of a doctrine (be it what it may) which I call an assumption of infallibility. It is the undertaking to decide that question *for others*, without allowing them to hear what can be said on the contrary side. And I denounce and reprobate that pretension not the less, if put forth on the side of my most solemn convictions. However positive any one's persuasion may be, not only of the falsity but of the pernicious consequences – not only of the pernicious consequences, but (to adopt expressions which I altogether condemn) the immorality and impiety of an opinion; yet if, in pursuance of that private judgment, though backed by the public judgment of his country or his contemporaries, he prevents the opinion from being heard in its defence, he assumes infallibility. And so far from the assumption being less objectionable or less dangerous because the opinion is called immoral or impious, this is the case of all others in which it is most fatal. These are exactly the occasions on which the men of one generation commit those dreadful mistakes which excite the astonishment and horror of posterity. It is among such that we find the instances memorable in history, when the arm of the law has been employed to root out the best men and the noblest doctrines.

John Stuart Mill, *On Liberty* (1859)

Censorship in action

What King Solomon was doing with all those women wouldn't be tolerated in San Francisco.

Police chief, prosecuting the publisher of Allen Ginsberg's
Howl and Other Poems in 1957, when asked if his standards
for obscenity wouldn't apply to the Bible

When Napoleon was starting for his campaign in Russia, he ordered the proof-sheets of a forthcoming book, about which there had been some disagreement among the censors of the press, to be put into his carriage, so that he might decide for himself what suppressions it might be necessary to make. 'Je m'ennuie en route; je lirai ces volumes, et j'écrirai de Mayence ce qu'il y aura à faire' . . . By the Emperor's command a few excisions were made.

Lytton Strachey, 'Madame du Deffand' (1913)

Their *Liberties* in the Following Particulars are intolerable. *viz*. Their *Swearing, Profainness*, and *Lewd Application of Scripture*; Their *Abuse* of the *Clergy*; Their *making* their *Top Characters Libertines*, and giving them *Success* in their *Debauchery*.

Jeremy Collier makes the case against contemporary playwrights in
A Short View of the Immorality and Profaneness of the English Stage (1698)

Many [French and Italian novels] are little better than histories of brothels and prostitutes, in these lust-cursed nations. How often have we found in these villainous stories, heroines, lovely, excellent, cultivated, wealthy, and charming in every way, who have for their lovers married men; or, after marriage, lovers flock about the charming wife, enjoying privileges belonging only to the husband! How often does the young wife in these accursed stories have a lover more wealthy and accomplished than the one to whom she has plighted her love! Clandestine meetings are described, and plots and conspiracies to put the husband out of the way are not infrequent.

What is the lesson to the young? A light estimate upon maiden virtue and marriage vows. A putting of vile thoughts and suggestions into the minds of the young. Sowing the seeds of lust.

Anthony Comstock, *Traps for the Young* (1884)

If a film gives me a funny feeling, I know it is dirty; but if I feel nothing, I know it is culture.

Singapore film censor, quoted in *Comic Cuts* (1970)

We are not censors. We just tell the exhibitors what pictures they can't show.

Film censor in Pasadena, quoted in *Comic Cuts* (1970)

Censorship as mutilation

I managed to get published the little cheap French edition, photographed down from the original, and offered at sixty francs. English publishers urge me to make an expurgated edition, promising large returns ... and insisting that I should show the public that here is a fine novel, apart from all 'purple' and all 'words'. So I begin to be tempted and start in to expurgate. But impossible! I might as well try to clip my own nose into shape with scissors. The book bleeds.

And in spite of all antagonism I put forth the novel as an honest, healthy book, necessary for us to-day. The words that shock so much at first don't shock at all after a while. Is this because the mind is depraved by habit? Not a bit. It is that the words merely shocked the eye, they never shocked the mind at all. People without minds may go on being shocked, but they don't matter. People with minds realize that they aren't shocked, and never really were: and they experience a sense of relief.

D. H. Lawrence, *A Propos of Lady Chatterley's Lover* (1930)

Gentility and self-censorship

Since the author of *Tom Jones* was buried, no writer of fiction among us has been permitted to depict to his utmost power a MAN. We must drape him, and give him a certain conventional simper. Society will not tolerate the Natural in our Art. Many ladies have remonstrated and subscribers left me, because, in the course of the story, I described a young man resisting and affected by temptation . . . A little more frankness than is customary has been attempted in this story; with no bad desire on the writer's part, it is hoped, and with no ill consequence to any reader.

William Makepeace Thackeray, Preface to
The History of Pendennis (1848–50)

The British mamma is determined that her daughter shall know nothing of life until she is married; at all events, that if she should learn anything, there should be no proof of her knowledge lying about the place – a book would be a proof . . . And as we are a thoroughly practical nation, the work is done thoroughly; root and branch are swept away, and we begin on a fresh basis, just as if Shakespeare and Ben Jonson had never existed. A novelist may say, 'I do not wish to enter into those pretty schoolrooms. I agree with you, my book is not fit reading for young girls; but does this prove I have written an immoral book?' The librarian answers, 'I cater for the masses, and the masses are young unmarried women who are supposed to know but one side of life. I cannot therefore take your book.' And so it comes to pass that English literature is sacrificed on the altar of Hymen.

George Moore, *Literature at Nurse or Circulating Morals* (1885)

Becoming a living book

Nowhere is there an image of a literary seduction more haunting than that of Nadezhda Mandelstam, the invisible woman, cradling for twenty years the saucepan containing the scraps of her dead husband's verse while the body of his writing was stored in her mind. These years of waiting and hiding she called 'my life in the tomb', and like this, with [Osip] Mandelstam's words entombed inside her, the poet's widow wandered across the largest space on earth in her ceaseless journey from one dull town to another: a living book.

Frances Wilson, *Literary Seductions* (1999)

LIFE-CHANGING BOOKS

How many a man has dated a new era in his life from the
reading of a book.

Henry David Thoreau, Walden (1854)

*There are books that have had a decisive impact on individual lives
and books that have changed the world. (And there are writers who
are convinced their world-shaking works are about to effect a revolution in human consciousness right up until the day they get remain-
dered.) Books have called attention to injustices, inspired political
movements and banished dangerous ignorance. In darkest days books
have kept alive hopes of freedom or defined the values people are
fighting or dying for. They have even helped liberate slaves.*

*This section celebrates the world-changing impact of books. But
it also brings together testimonies of lives changed by particular
books, sometimes very ordinary or surprising books, which suggested new possibilities, values or dreams. Books have often cut
through religious dogmas, sexual attitudes or received political wisdom and enabled people to remake their lives by embracing other
behaviours and beliefs. There are cases of a single book curing
depression, inspiring a lifetime's work – or even causing reader to
fall in love with writer.*

Books and the call of freedom

We must be free or die, who speak the tongue
That Shakespeare spake . . .

William Wordsworth, Morning Post, 17 September 1803

The frequent hearing of my mistress reading the Bible aloud, for she often read aloud when her husband was absent, awakened my curiosity in respect to this *mystery* of reading, and roused in me the desire to learn. Up to this time I had known nothing of this wonderful art, and my ignorance and inexperience of what it could do for me, as well as my confidence in my mistress, emboldened me to ask her to teach me to read. With an unconsciousness and inexperience equal to my own, she readily consented, and in an incredibly short time, by her kind assistance, I had mastered the alphabet and could spell words of three or four letters ... Master Hugh was astounded beyond measure and, probably for the first time, proceeded to unfold to his wife the true philosophy of the slave system, and the peculiar rules necessary in the nature of the case to be observed in the management of human chattels. Of course he forbade her to give me any further instruction, telling her in the first place that to do so was unlawful, as it was also unsafe; 'for', said he, 'if you give a nigger an inch he will take an ell. Learning will spoil the best nigger in the world ...'

Frederick Douglass, a freed slave, wakes up to the importance
of learning in *Life and Times of Frederick Douglass* (1881)

Whoever feels the value of literature, whoever sees the central part it plays in the development of human history, must also see the life and death necessity of resisting totalitarianism, whether it is imposed on us from without or within.

George Orwell, 'Literature and Totalitarianism' (1941)

Participation in this youth movement [a leftist movement called the Jung Vondervogel] also happened to introduce me to Freud and psychoanalysis. That sex need not be a taboo area and that sexual anxiety can be relieved and sexual repression undone were terribly liberating notions for a middle-class adolescent in Vienna at that time. This was personal liberation, but the writings of the free school movement represented social liberation, since it offered an alternative to the regime under which I chafed. It offered a freer, better, and more humane way to educate the young – like me. Freud seemed to offer freedom from the sexual restraints and anxieties from which I, a typically inhibited middle-class adolescent, suffered; and the combination of sexual liberation and educational reform became a revelation, since both suggested that I need not suffer from what severely oppressed me. What greater service can books give us than to free us from anger and anxiety about possible school failure and the nightmares of sexual fear?

Bruno Bettelheim, 'Essential Books in One's Life' (1987–8)

Books cannot be killed by fire. People die, but books never die. No man and no force can abolish memory . . . In this war, we know, books are weapons.

F. D. Roosevelt, message to the American
Booksellers' Association, 23 April 1942

There was a library at school. What treasures I imagined behind the glass panels of the bookcases! When I came home and said that the teacher had given me permission to sign up for the library, [her Orthodox Jewish] Father stopped eating his dinner and declared that under no circumstances was I to read any Polish books . . . Mother came to my aid. Together we agreed that I would sign up for the library without Father's knowledge. And that is what I did.

I devoted myself to reading with a passion. Within the red and blue covers of the library's books I found an enchanted world, filled with regal characters involved in wondrous tales that completely captured my young mind . . .

The Polish books gave me much to think about. I saw life from a different perspective. For the first time I saw another kind of existence. I learned about the extraordinary heroism of historical figures, and I also saw their private lives.

I discovered the existence of a new feeling – the feeling of love.

'Esther', in J. Shandler (ed.), *Awakening Lives* (2002)

Books which led to love . . .

One day we reading were for our delight
    Of Launcelot, how Love did him enthrall.
    Alone we were and without any fear.
Full many a time our eyes together drew
    That reading, and drove the color from our faces;
    But one point only was it that o'ercame us.
Whenas we read of the much longed-for smile
    Being by such a noble lover kissed,
    This one, who n'er from me shall be divided,
Kissed me upon the mouth all palpitating.
    Galeotto was the book and he who wrote it.
    That day no further did we read therein.

Francesca di Rimini describing the fatal kiss that doomed
her and her lover Paolo, in Dante's *Inferno*, Canto v
(translated by Henry Wadsworth Longfellow, 1886)

I love your verses with all my heart, dear Miss Barrett . . . since the day last week when I first read your poems, I quite laugh to remember how I have been turning and turning again in my mind what I should be able to tell you of their effect upon me . . . I do, as I say, love these books with all my heart – and I love you too: do you know that I was once not very far from seeing – really seeing you? Mr Kenyon said to

me one morning 'Would you like to see Miss Barrett?' – then
he went to announce me – then he returned . . . you were too
unwell – and now it is many years ago – and I feel as at some
untoward passage in my travels – as if I had been close, so
close, to some world's-wonder in chapel or crypt, only a
screen to push and I might have entered, but there was some
slight . . . so it now seems . . . slight and just-sufficient bar to
admission; and the half-opened door shut, and I went home
my thousands of miles, and the sight was never to be!

First letter of Robert Browning to Elizabeth Barrett, 10 January 1845

The political influence of Swift

When Swift is considered as an author, it is just to estimate
his powers by their effects. In the reign of Queen Anne he
turned the stream of popularity against the Whigs, and must
be confessed to have dictated for a time the political opinions
of the English nation. In the succeeding reign he delivered
Ireland from plunder and oppression; and shewed that wit
confederated with truth, had such force as authority was
unable to resist. He said truly of himself that Ireland 'was his
debtor'. It was from the time when he first began to patronize
the Irish, that they may date their riches and prosperity. He
taught them first to know their own interest, their weight,
and their strength, and gave them spirit to assert that equal-
ity with their fellow subjects to which they have ever since
been making vigorous advances, and to claim those rights
which they have at last established. Nor can they be charged
with ingratitude to their benefactor; for they reverenced him
as a guardian, and obeyed him as a dictator.

Dr Samuel Johnson, *Lives of the Poets*, vol. II (1780)

133

Shelley's schemes to reform human nature

[Scythrop Glowry] wrote and published a treatise, in which his meanings were carefully wrapt up in the monk's hood of transcendental technology, but filled with hints of matter deep and dangerous, which he thought would set the whole nation in a ferment; and he awaited the result in awful expectation, as a miner who has fired a train awaits the explosion of a rock. However, he listened and heard nothing; for the explosion, if any ensued, was not sufficiently loud to shake a single leaf of the ivy on the towers of Nightmare Abbey; and some months afterwards he received a letter from his bookseller, informing him that only seven copies had been sold, and concluding with a polite request for the balance.

Scythrop did not despair. 'Seven copies', he thought, 'have been sold. Seven is a mystical number, and the omen is good. Let me find the seven purchasers of my seven copies, and they shall be the seven golden candle-sticks with which I will illuminate the world.'

A satirical portrait of Shelley, in Thomas Love Peacock,
Nightmare Abbey (1818)

The impact of childhood reading

My father had left a small collection of books in a little room upstairs, to which I had access (for it adjoined my own), and which nobody else in our house ever troubled. From that blessed little room, Roderick Random, Peregrine Pickle, Humphrey Clinker, Tom Jones, the Vicar of Wakefield, Don Quixote, Gil Blas, and Robinson Crusoe, came out, a glorious host, to keep me company. They kept alive my fancy, and my hope of something beyond that place and time.

Charles Dickens, *David Copperfield* (1849–50)

One gift the Fairies gave me: (Three
They commonly bestowed of yore)
The Love of Books, the Golden Key
That opens the Enchanted Door;
Behind it BLUEBEARD lurks and o'er
And o'er doth JACK his Giants kill,
And there is all ALADDIN's store, –
The Books I loved, I love them still!

Andrew Lang, 'The Ballad of the Bookworm' (1887)

I was an omnivorous reader and devoured science books, but then I devoured everything. I read the wonderful George Gamow Mr Tompkins books, with their vivid visualizations of quantum theory and relativity, which still provide me with my mental images of physics. I read Eve Curie's biography of her mother *Marie Curie*, many times over. (I wonder whether there is any woman in science today who didn't read *Marie Curie* many times over.)

Cognitive scientist Alison Gopnik,
'A Midcentury Modern Education' (2004)

I had become fond of Longfellow's *Saga of King Olaf*: fond of it in a casual, shallow way for its story and its vigorous rhythms. But then, and quite different from such pleasures, and like a voice from far more distant regions, there came a moment when I idly turned the pages of the book and found the unrhymed translation of *Tegner's Drapa* and read

> *I heard a voice that cried,*
> *Balder the beautiful*
> *Is dead, is dead –*

I knew nothing about Balder; but instantly I was uplifted into huge regions of northern sky, I desired with almost sickening intensity something never to be described (except that it is cold, spacious, severe, pale, and remote) and then . . . found myself at the very same moment already falling out of my desire and wishing I were back in it.

C. S. Lewis, Surprised By Joy (1955)

Maybe obsessive reading imprints a love of words in a child, and perhaps later assists the craft of writing. In particular, I wonder whether the formative influence that eventually led to my becoming a zoologist might have been a children's book: Hugh Lofting's *The Adventures of Doctor Dolittle*, which I read again and again, along with its numerous sequels. This series of books did not turn me on to science in any direct sense, but Dr Dolittle was a scientist, the world's greatest naturalist, and a thinker of restless curiosity. Long before either phrase was coined, he was a role model who raised my consciousness.

Richard Dawkins, 'Dolittle and Darwin' (2004)

> How am I to sing your praise,
> Happy chimney-corner days,
> Sitting safe in nursery nooks,
> Reading picture story-books?

Robert Louis Stevenson, 'Picture-books in Winter' (1885)

Joining 'the Penguin generation' in Baghdad

It was Pelican and later Penguin titles on which my literary and cultural education [in 1940s Baghdad] was to depend for some years since those first days of reading English. In those days, Penguins – and probably Pelicans too – used to come out in batches of ten at a time, and I remember spending hours browsing and weighing and agonizing before I was to decide which was to be the first of the batch to spend 30 *fils* on

– or the first two or three if I happened to have such incredible sums on me . . .

We had to do quite a good number of regular, almost daily visits to all bookshops and all the stores where books were sold, so that we could catch the consignments as they arrived – and sometimes it was a matter of two or three months before a ship arrived with the precious packages.

Nissim Rejwan, The Last Jews in Baghdad (2004)

A book which banished despair

I was reading, accidentally, Marmontel's *Memoirs*, and came to the passage which relates his father's death, the distressed position of the family, and the sudden inspiration which he, then a mere boy, felt and made them feel that he would be everything to them – would supply the place of all that they had lost. A vivid conception of this scene and its feelings came over me, and I was moved to tears. From this moment my burthen grew lighter. The oppression of the thought that all feeling was dead within me, was gone . . . I was not a stock or a stone . . . Relieved from my ever present sense of irremediable wretchedness, I gradually found that the ordinary incidents of life could again give me some pleasure; that I could again find enjoyment, not intense, but sufficient for cheerfulness, in sunshine and sky, in books, in conversation, in public affairs.

John Stuart Mill, Autobiography (1873)

Books to inspire a heroine

Mrs Morland was a very good woman, and wished to see her children every thing they ought to be: but her time was so much occupied in lying-in and teaching the little ones, that

137

her elder daughters were invariably left to shift for themselves; and it was not very wonderful that Catherine, who had
by nature nothing heroic about her, should prefer cricket,
base-ball, riding on horseback, and running about the country, at the age of fourteen, to books, or at least books of
information, for, provided that nothing like useful knowledge
could be gained from them, provided they were all story and
no reflection, she had never any objection to books at all. But
from fifteen to seventeen she was in training for a heroine; she
read all such works as heroines must read to supply their
memories with those quotations which are so serviceable and
so soothing in the vicissitudes of their eventful lives.

Jane Austen, *Northanger Abbey* (1818)

A book that inspired a narrative poem

Do you see this square old yellow Book, I toss
I' the air, and catch again, and twirl about
By the crumpled vellum covers, – pure crude fact
Secreted from a man's life when hearts beat hard,
And brains, high-blooded, ticked two centuries since?
Examine it yourselves! I found this book,
Gave a *lira* for it, eightpence English just,
(Mark the predestination!) when a Hand,
Always above my shoulder, pushed me once,
One day still fierce 'mid many a day struck calm,
Across a Square in Florence, crammed with booths,
Buzzing and blaze, noontide and market-time.

Robert Browning describes the chance find in an Italian market
which formed the basis for *The Ring and the Book* (1868–9)

Talismanic books

The few books in German that Henny must have brought with her as an exile to England are a small atlas, a couple of textbooks for learning English, a small volume of folksongs set to music for the lute, and three large, slim paperbacks illustrated with full-page black-and-white photographs: on modern German sculpture, on German baroque architecture and on the German countryside in the spring.

Five other books were in the trunk, but they have different provenances. One of them (in English) was published by Chatto & Windus in 1941: *The Rubaiyat of Omar Khayyám* translated by Edward FitzGerald. Two of them appear to be gifts given after the war: the poems of Michelangelo translated into German by Rilke, and a book on Dürer. The final two, and for me the puzzling ones, are two hardbound books in black: a Jewish Bible in German and a Jewish prayer-book, in German and Hebrew . . .

I treat them as talismans; I often dip into them. If only they could speak and tell me where they have been, what hands have held them, what insight or faith or peace they have brought and to whom, how they survived a bitter and desecrating time and by what circuitous means and ways they have come down to me, a quasi-agnostic Hindu.

Vikram Seth, *Two Lives* (2005)

READING EVERYWHERE

I should like the window to open onto the Lake of Geneva –
and there I'd sit and read all day like the picture of somebody reading.

John Keats, letter to his sister Fanny, 13 March 1819

*Many people love to read in bed. Today, one can do so in perfect
safety, but in the days of candles and wigs many a scholar risked
conflagration if he dozed off in mid-sentence. It took an ingenious
Chinese sage to attach his pigtail to a beam so that he was jerked
awake if drowsiness hovered . . .*

*There are cases of people so besotted with reading (or keen to dis-
play their sang-froid) that they took a book with them on the way
to the gallows. Many of us cart half a library on holiday with us,
although we usually come to realise that a single potboiler or book of
anecdotes is really best for the beach or after a hard day tramping
round museums or city streets. Yet in certain moods work, family,
food and sleep can seem nothing more than a conspiracy of tiresome
irritations designed to curtail our reading time. This section celebrates
reading in unusual places and circumstances – and the ruses that
readers have adopted to escape encroaching children or the boss's eye . . .*

*Hazards abound. It can be genuinely dangerous to try to read
while crossing roads or walking in hilly terrain. And those easily
moved to tears can get some very funny looks if they start crying
over a poignant passage in Piccadilly.*

Born readers

The born reader reads anywhere, anywhen, by day or night,
by the light of the moon and the stars, or even, so I have heard,
by lightning or the *aurora borealis*; by sunlight and candlelight,

gaslight or electricity; on land or sea, walking or riding, standing or sitting or lying in bed; on chairs or sofas, on couches, in hammocks, in baths and at stool; on board ships, in punts, rowing-boats, and canoes; up trees; on ladders; on omnibuses, or bicycles, in railway trains, or automobiles, cabs, carriages, tram-way cars, jaunting cars, buggies, balloons, airships or aeroplanes, or any other vehicle for sea, land or air; in hospitals, penitentiaries, prisons; in kitchens, parlours, caves, arbours, etc.; on the backs of horses, camels, mules, asses, elephants . . . during air raids and bombardments, wars, revolutions and pestilences; in joy and sorrow, health and sickness.

Holbrook Jackson, The Anatomy of Bibliomania (1950)

At the morning distribution of chores, Private X . . . always volunteers for the least popular, most unpleasant chore, a chore usually handed out as a punishment and which can stain even the most glorious reputation: the legendary, infamous, unspeakable *bog duty* . . .

Hours go by. They think he's got lost. They almost forget about him, then do forget him. But at the end of the morning he reappears, clicking his heels to report to the sergeant-major: 'Latrines impeccable, sir!' The sergeant-major takes back the mop and broom with a questioning expression he never puts into words . . . The soldier salutes, about-turns and retreats, taking his secret away with him.

His secret is quite a weight in the right-hand pocket of his fatigues: the 1,900 pages which make up the complete works of Nikolai Gogol in the Pléiade edition. A quarter of an hour with a mop in return for a morning reading Gogol . . . Every morning for two winter months, sitting comfortably in his double-locked throne room, Private X has been flying high above the demands of military service.

Daniel Pennac, Comme un roman (1992)

Reading while eating

I had another half-hour, and sometimes an hour's reading or study of language, at from one to two o'clock, the time of dinner – usually eating my food with a spoon, after I had cut it in pieces, and having my eyes on a book all the time.

> Thomas Cooper, an autodidact Victorian cobbler,
> *The Life and Times of Thomas Cooper* (1872)

Observe, there comes to you, by the Kendal wagon tomorrow, the illustrious 5th of November, a box, containing the Miltons, the strange American Bible, with White's brief note, to which you will attend; Baxter's 'Holy Commonwealth', for which you stand indebted to me 3s 6d; an odd volume of Montaigne, being of no use to me, I having the whole; certain books belonging to Wordsworth, as do also the strange thick-hoofed shoes, which are very much admired in London. All these sundries I commend to your most strenuous looking after. If you find the Miltons in certain parts dirtied and soiled with a crumb of right Gloucester blacked in the candle (my usual supper), or peradventure a stray ash of tobacco wafted into the creases, look to that passage more especially: depend upon it, it contains good matter.

> Charles Lamb, letter to Samuel Taylor Coleridge, 4 November 1802

Reading on the stairs

At seven years [the poet Francis Thompson] was reading poetry and, overwhelmed by feelings of which he knew not the meaning, had found his way to the heart of Shakespeare and Coleridge ... Already seeking the highway and the highway's seclusion, he would carry his book to the stairs, where, away from the constraint of chairs and tables and the unemotional flatness of the floor, his sister Mary remembers him. It is on that household highway, where the voices and noises of the house, and the footsteps of passengers on the pavement beyond the dark front door, come and pass quickly into other regions, that the child meditates and learns. There he may contract the habit of loneliness, populate his fancy with the creatures of fear; and gather about him a company of thoughts that will be his intimates until the end.

Everard Meynell, *The Life of Francis Thompson* (1913)

Reading in bed

Observation has convinced me that all good and true book-lovers practise the pleasing and improving avocation of reading in bed ... [The evidence of his writings] demonstrates beyond doubt that Cicero made a practice of reading in bed. Why, I can almost see him now, propped up in his couch, unrolling scroll after scroll of his favorite literature, and enjoying it mightily too, which enjoyment is interrupted now and then by the occasions which the noble reader takes to mutter maledictions upon the slave who has let the lamp run low of oil or has neglected to trim the wick.

Eugene Field, *The Love Affairs of a Bibliomaniac* (1896)

A house with seven or eight children on one floor is a fine opportunity for the display of patience on the part of a 'student' or an earnest reader. Get into bed for warmth and then the luxury of an unbroken reading was a treat that compensated for any privations, and lifted me for the time being into another world.

Thomas Wood, an autodidact Yorkshire engineer,
The Autobiography of Thomas Wood (1956)

Give me Books, fruit, French wine and fine weather and a little music out of doors, played by somebody I do not know.

John Keats, letter to his sister Fanny, 28 August 1819

Another couple had an infant, aged three, and this infant had a rather fierce grandmother, and this grandmother read a great deal. She and I stood alone for literature. She would stay at home with the infant while the intermediate generation was away larking. She was always reading the same book. It was a thick book, with a glossy coloured cover displaying some scene in which homicide and passion were mingled; its price, new, was sixpence halfpenny, and its title was simply and magnificently, 'Borgia!' with a note of exclamation after it. She confined herself to 'Borgia!' She was tireless with 'Borgia!' She went home to Paris reading 'Borgia!' It was a shocking hotel, so different from the literary hotels of Switzerland, Bournemouth, and Scarborough, where all the guests read Meredith and Walter Pater. I ought to have been ashamed to be seen in such a place. My only excuse is that the other two hotels in the remote little village were just as bad, probably worse.

Arnold Bennett, 'Holiday Reading' (1910)

I would sooner read the catalogue of the Army and Navy Stores or Bradshaw's *Guide* than nothing at all, and indeed I have spent many delightful hours over both these works. At one time I never went out without a second-hand bookseller's list in my pocket. I know no reading more fruity . . . like the dope-fiend who cannot move from place to place without taking with him a plentiful supply of his deadly balm I never venture far without a sufficiency of reading matter . . . I

145

have learnt my lesson. Once, imprisoned by illness for three months in a hill-town in Java, I . . . was obliged to buy the schoolbooks from which intelligent Javanese, I suppose, acquired knowledge of French and German. So I read again after five-and-twenty years the frigid plays of Goethe, the fables of La Fontaine and the tragedies of the tender and exact Racine. I have the greatest admiration for Racine, but I admit that to read his plays one after another requires a certain effort in a person who is suffering from colitis.

Somerset Maugham, *The Book Bag* (1932)

Near thirty years ago I was thinking 'How is it no horse ever stumbles when I am reading?' (History, poetry, and philosophy I commonly read on horseback, having other employment at other times.) No account can possibly be given but this: because I throw the reins on his neck. I then set myself to observe; and I aver that, in riding above a hundred thousand miles, I scarce ever remember a horse (except two, that would fall head over heels any way) to fall over, or make a considerable stumble, while I rode with *a slack rein.*

The Journal of the Rev. Charles Wesley (1774), March 1770

It is wonderful how conducive to reading I found the stuffy smoking-rooms of the little steamers that dart like water-spiders from one landing to another on the Italian Lakes.

A. Edward Newton, *Amenities of Book-Collecting* (1920)

I have a record of G. K. Chesterton being espied on Ilkley Moor, in Yorkshire, one cold day in spring, *leaning in the rain against a budding tree, absorbed in the pages of a little red book*; and I heard that same author tell how once, whilst riding in a hansom cab, reading one of his own admirable essays, he observed a commotion in the street through which the cab was passing and, to his astonishment, discovered that his situation had been strangely and suddenly translated, for instead of being seated comfortably reading in the cab, the cab was upside down and he sat beneath it in the road, still reading.

Holbrook Jackson, The Anatomy of Bibliomania (1950)

Being read to – in the nursery and the jungle

There [in 'the black friendly labyrinth' of her grandmother's gowns] one nestled for hours while she told stories. The book of Genesis, myths of Greece, the Siegfried sagas, the Seven Kings of Rome, Tasso, Dante, Goethe, came to me in this good way, not arid noises from a mechanical cavern, or black and white deserts of print, but warm with the person of the teller, modulated with the inflections of a voice that meant safety and kindness, so that the childhood of the world merged with my own and lies there entranced in the same afternoon light that melted into twilight, and gradually dimmed the ivory face and left the voice almost alone to call up pageant after pageant.

Freya Stark, Traveller's Prelude (1950)

At the end of the first day [Mr Todd, the illiterate old man who has nursed Tony Last back to health in the Amazonian jungle] said, 'You read beautifully, with a far better accent than the black man. And you explain it better. It is almost as though my father were here again.' And always at the end of a session he thanked his guest courteously. 'I enjoyed that *very* much. It was an extremely distressing chapter. But, if I remember it rightly, it will all turn out well.'

By the time they were in the second volume, however, the novelty of the old man's delight had begun to wane, and Tony

147

was feeling strong enough to be restless. He touched more than once on the subject of his departure, asking about canoes and rains and the possibility of finding guides. But Mr Todd seemed obtuse and paid no attention to these hints.

One day, running his thumb through the pages of *Bleak House* that remained to be read, Tony said, 'We still have a lot to get through. I hope I shall be able to finish it before I go.'

'Oh yes,' said Mr Todd. 'Do not disturb yourself about that. You will have time to finish it, my friend.'

For the first time Tony noticed something slightly menacing in his host's manner.

Evelyn Waugh, A Handful of Dust (1934)

Reading instead of fishing

For a whole day together, have I lain
Down by thy side, O Derwent! murmuring stream
On the hot stones, and in the glaring sun,
And there have I read, devouring as I read,
Defrauding the day's glory, desperate!

William Wordsworth, The Prelude (1850)

Some fishermen are great readers out of doors, with a taste that argues (unless the result of gross insensitivity) no mean judgment and knowledge of books. To know what will stand the fierce outdoor light that hopelessly demeans the average book is a literary achievement. In this way the sun is a true critic, and the only present test of immortality.

Edward Thomas, 'Digressions on Fish and Fishing' (1902)

Reading during war

He [the French novelist Stendhal] was at Moscow in 1812, and he accompanied the army through the horrors of the retreat. When the conflagration had broken out in the city he had abstracted from one of the deserted palaces a finely bound copy of the *Facéties* of Voltaire; the book helped to divert his mind as he lay crouched by the camp-fire through the terrible nights that followed; but, as his companions showed their disapproval of anyone who could smile over Akakia and Pompignan in such a situation, one day he left the red-morocco volume behind him in the snow.

Lytton Strachey, 'Henri Beyle' (1914)

A crafty tip for reading at work

Lay the book on your lap directly beneath your middle desk drawer. The disaster-area desktop is not compulsory for this technique, although various reports must be placed in front of you to complete the pose. As a boss or coworker approaches your desk, merely pull your chair up quickly into the chair well and make like you are crunching numbers or doing whatever it is that you do. But remember: the hands must be placed on the desktop at all times to remove suspicion.

Tom Raabe, *Biblioholism* (1991)

SOURCES AND ACKNOWLEDGEMENTS

Every effort has been made to contact copyright holders; in the event of an inadvertent omission or error, the editorial department should be notified at The Folio Society Ltd, 44 Eagle Street, London WC1R 4FS.

Addison, Joseph, *Tatler*, vol. CCLVII (18 March 1709).

Anon., 'Old Books', in *Ballads of Books*, ed. James Branden Matthews (1887).

———, 'It's a Long Way to Tipperary', French trans., in John Julius Norwich, *Still More Christmas Crackers* (London, Viking, 2000).

Arnold, Matthew, *On Translating Homer* (1861).

———, 'The Function of Criticism at the Present Time', *Essays in Criticism* (1865).

Aubrey, John, *Brief Lives*, 'set down between the Years 1669 & 1696', ed. Andrew Clark (1898).

Austen, Jane, *Northanger Abbey* (1818).

———, *Persuasion* (1818).

Bacon, Francis, *An Advertisement Touching the Controversies of the Church of England* (1589–91).

———, *Advancement of Learning* (1605).

Bagehot, Walter, 'The First Edinburgh Reviewers', *National Review* (October 1855).

———, 'The Metaphysical Basis of Tolerance', *Contemporary Review* (April 1874).

Baker, Nicholson, article first published in *New Yorker* (1983); reprinted in *The Size of Thoughts: Essays and Other Lumber* (London, Chatto & Windus, 1996). Copyright © 1983 Nicholson Baker. Reproduced by permission of the author

c/o Rogers, Coleridge & White Ltd.

Baxter, John, *A Pound of Paper: Confessions of a Book Addict* (London, Doubleday, 2002). Copyright © 2002 by John Baxter. Reproduced by permission of The Random House Group Ltd and St Martins Press.

Beach, Sylvia, *Shakespeare and Company* (New York, Harcourt Brace, 1959). Copyright © 1956, 1959 by Sylvia Beach. Reproduced by permission of the author's estate.

Beecher, Henry Ward, *Star Papers; or, Experiences of Art and Nature* (1855).

Beerbohm, Max, 'Books within Books', in *And Even Now* (1920). Reproduced by permission of Berlin Associates.

Belloc, Hilaire, 'On Not Reading Books', 'On Translation', in *A Conversation with An Angel and Other Essays* (London, Jonathan Cape, 1928). Copyright © The Estate of Hilaire Belloc 1976. Reproduced by permission of PFD (www.pfd.co.uk) on behalf of The Estate of Hilaire Belloc.

Benjamin, Walter, 'Unpacking My Library: A Talk on Book Collecting', trans. Harry Zohn, in *Illuminations* (New York, Harcourt, Brace and World, 1968; London, Jonathan Cape, 1970); reprinted in Michael W. Jennings (ed.), *Walter Benjamin: Selected Writings*, vol. II: *1927–1934* (Cambridge, Mass., The

Belknap Press of Harvard University Press, 1996–2005). Copyright © 1999 by the President and Fellows of Harvard College. Reproduced by permission of The Random House Group Ltd., Harcourt, Inc. and Harvard University Press.

Bennett, Arnold, 'Holiday Reading', *New Age* (4 August 1910); reprinted in *Books and Persons* (1917).

Bennett, Jesse Lee, *What Books Do for You* (1923).

Bennoch, Francis, 'My Books' (1878), in *Ballads of Books*, ed. James Branden Matthews (1887).

Bentley, Richard, cited in Dr Samuel Johnson, 'Pope', in *Lives of the Poets*, vol. III (1791).

Betjeman, John, 'In Westminster Abbey', in *Old Lights for New Chancels* (London, John Murray, 1940). Reproduced by permission of John Murray (Publishers) Ltd.

Bettelheim, Bruno, 'Essential Books in One's Life' (1987–8), reprinted in *Recollections and Reflections* (London, Thames & Hudson, 1990). Copyright © 1956 . . . 1989 by Bruno Bettelheim. Reproduced by kind permission of the Estate of Bruno Bettelheim and Thames & Hudson London Ltd.

Bierce, Ambrose, *The Devil's Dictionary* (1911).

Borges, Jorge Luis, 'The Library of Babel', trans. Andrew Hurley, in *Collected Fictions* (New York, Viking Penguin, 1998). Copyright © Maria Kodoma, 1998; translation copyright © Penguin Putnam Inc., 1998. Reproduced by permission of Penguin Books Ltd; Viking Penguin, a division of Penguin Group (USA) Inc.; and the Penguin Group (Canada), a division of Pearson Canada Inc.

Boswell, James, *London Journal 1762–1763*, with an Introduction and notes by Frederick A. Pottle (Heinemann, 1950).

——, *The Life of Samuel Johnson* (1791).

Brierley, Ben, *Home Memories and Recollections of a Life* (1886), quoted in David Vincent, *Bread, Knowledge and Freedom: A Study of Nineteenth-Century Working-Class Autobiography* (London, Europa Publications, 1981).

Browning, Robert, *The Ring and the Book*, I.33–44 (1868–9).

——, 'Development', in *Asolando* (1889).

Burton, John Hill, *The Book-Hunter* (2nd edn, 1885).

Bury, Richard de, *Philobiblon* (1345), trans. Ernest Chester Thomas (1888).

Butler, Samuel, 'Ramblings in Cheapside', *Universal Review* (December 1890); reprinted in *Essays on Life, Art and Science* (1904).

Byron, Lord George Gordon Noel, *English Bards and Scotch Reviewers* (1809).

Callimachus, 'Heraclitus', trans. William Cory, in *Ionica* (1858).

Carlyle, Thomas, speech addressing a meeting to set up the London Library, *Examiner* (28 June 1840).

——, 'The Hero as Man of Letters', in *On Heroes, Hero-Worship and the Heroic in History* (1841).

——, *Reminiscences*, ed. James Anthony Froude (1881).

Cobbett, William, *Year's Residence, in the United States of America* (1818).

Cobden-Sanderson, T. J., 'The Threefold Purpose of the Doves Press', part of the first Doves Press *Catalogue Raisonné* (1908).

——, *The Journals of Thomas-James Cobden-Sanderson 1879–1922*, 2 vols (1926).

Collier, Jeremy, *A Short View of the Immorality and Profaneness of the English Stage* (1698).

Comstock, Anthony, *Traps for the Young* (1884).

Cooper, Thomas, *The Life and Times of Thomas Cooper, written by himself* (1872), quoted in David Vincent, *Bread, Knowledge and Freedom* (London, Europa Publications, 1981).

Cory, William, 'Heraclitus' (translation of Callimachus), in *Ionica* (1858).

Coward, Noël, 'Useless Useful Phrases', in *The Complete Lyrics of Noël Coward* (London, Methuen Drama, an imprint of A & C Black Ltd, 1998). Copyright © The Estate of Noël Coward. Reproduced by permission of Methuen Drama, an imprint of A & C Black Ltd.

Cowley, Abraham, 'The Book Humbly presenting it selfe to the Universitie Librarie at Oxford', in *Verses, Lately Written Upon Several Occasions* (1663).

Crabbe, George, *The Library* (1781).

Daniel, Samuel, 'Concerning the Honor of Books', Prefatory poem to the 2nd edn of Florio's translation of Montaigne (1613).

Dante, *Inferno*, Canto v, ll. 127–38, trans. Henry Wadsworth Longfellow (1886).

Dawkins, Richard, 'Dolittle and Darwin', in *When We Were Kids: How a Child Becomes a Scientist*, ed. John Brockman (London, Jonathan Cape, 2004). Reproduced by permission of Richard Dawkins and Brockman, Inc.

De Quincey, Thomas, 'Anglo-German Dictionaries', *London Magazine* (1823); reprinted in *Uncollected Writings*, ed. James Hogg, vol. II (1890).

Dibdin, Reverend Thomas Frognall, *The BIBLIOMANIA or Book Madness* (1809); reprinted, with an Introduction and Notes by Peter Danckwerts (Richmond, Tiger of the Stripe, 2004).

Dickens, Charles, *David Copperfield* (1849–50).

Dickinson, Emily, Poem 1263 (*c.*1873), in *Letters of Emily Dickinson*, ed. Mable Loomis Todd (1894).

D'Israeli, Isaac, *Curiosities of Literature* (1791).

Dobson, Austin, 'My Books' (1885), in *Ballads of Books*, ed. James Branden Matthews (1887).

Douglass, Frederick, *Life and Times of Frederick Douglass* (1881).

Dryden, John, dedication to the *Aeneïs* (1697).

Eliot, George, 'Silly Novels by Lady Novelists', *Westminster Review* (October 1856).

Euripides, *Suppliant Women*, quoted at the head of Milton's 'Areopagitica' (1644).

Ferriar, John, *The Bibliomania: An Epistle, to Richard Heber, Esq.* (1809).

Fertiault, F., 'A Domestic Event', in *Ballads of Books*, ed. Andrew Lang (1888).

Field, Eugene, *The Love Affairs of a Bibliomaniac* (1896).

Findlater, Richard, *Comic Cuts: A Bedside Sampler of Censorship in Action* (London, André Deutsch, 1970). Reproduced by permission of Carlton Publishing Group.

Fitzgerald, Penelope, *The Bookshop* (London, Duckworth, 1978). Reproduced by permission of Harper Collins Ltd.

Forster, E. M., 'My Library', in *Two Cheers for Democracy* (London, Edward Arnold, 1951). Copyright © 1951 by E. M. Forster and renewed 1979 by Donald Parry. Reproduced by permission of the Provost and Scholars of King's College, Cambridge, the Society of Authors as the Literary Representatives of the Estate of E. M. Forster and Harcourt, Inc.

Franklin, Benjamin, 'An Apology for Printers' (1731).

Gibbon, Edward, *The History of the
Decline and Fall of the Roman Empire*
(1776–88).

———, *Memoirs of My Life* (1796).

Gill, Eric, *An Essay on Typography* (London,
Sheed & Ward, 1931). Copyright © The
Estate of the Artist/Bridgeman Art
Library. Reprinted with permission.

Gissing, George, *New Grub Street* (1891).

———, *The Private Papers of Henry Ryecroft* (1905).

———, 'Christopherson', in *The House of
Cobwebs* (1906).

Gladstone, William Ewart, *On Books and
the Housing of Them* (1898).

Golding, Arthur, Preface to his translation
of Ovid's *Metamorphoses* (1567).

Gopnik, Alison, 'A Midcentury Modern
Education', in *When We Were Kids: How a
Child Becomes a Scientist*, ed. John Brock-
man (London, Jonathan Cape, 2004).
Reproduced by permission of Alison
Gopnik and Brockman, Inc.

Gosse, Edmund, Introduction to *Gossip in a
Library* (1891).

Hanff, Helene, *84, André Deutsch*, 1971). Copyright © 1970 by Helene Hanff. Grateful
acknowledgement is made to Moyer
Bell and to the Carlton Publishing
Group for permission to reproduce
material from this book.

Hava, J. G., *Arabic–English Dictionary*
(Beirut, Catholic Press, 1964).

Haydon, Benjamin Robert, *The Autobiog-
raphy and Memoirs of Benjamin Robert
Haydon, 1786–1846*, ed. Alexander P. D.
Penrose (1927).

Hazlitt, William, 'On Reading Old Books',
London Magazine (February 1821).

———, 'Mr Wordsworth', in *The Spirit
of the Age* (1825).

Henley, William Ernest, 'Villon's Straight
Tip to All Cross Coves', Appendix to
Works, vol. II (1908).

Hitchings, Henry, *Dr Johnson's Dictionary:
The Extraordinary Story of the Book that
Defined the World* (London, John Murray, 2005). Copyright © Henry Hitchings 2005. Reproduced by permission
of John Murray (Publishers) Ltd and
Farrar, Straus and Giroux.

Hofstadter, Douglas, *Le Ton beau de Marot:
In Praise of the Music of Language* (London, Bloomsbury, 1997). Reproduced by
permission of Bloomsbury Publishing
and Basic Books.

Horace, Ode I.5, individual stanzas trans.
by William Boscawen, Patrick Branwell
Bronte, William Duncombe and
Christopher Smart, in Ronald Storrs, *Ad
Pyrrham* (London, Oxford University
Press, 1959).

Housman, A. E., 'Fragment of a Greek
Tragedy', *Bromsgrovian* (June 1883).

———, 'Diffugere Nives' (1897), translation of Horace, *Odes* IV.7, reprinted in
More Poems (1936).

———, *The Name and Nature of Poetry*
(Leslie Stephen Lecture, Cambridge,
1933). Reproduced by permission of the
Society of Authors as the Literary Representative of the Estate of A. E. Housman.

Hubbard, Elbert, *The Roycroft Dictionary
Concocted by Ali Baba and the Bunch on
Rainy Days* (1914).

Hunt, Leigh, 'My Books', in *The Literary
Examiner* (1823).

———, 'A Word on Translation from the
Poets', in *The Indicator* (1833).

Irving, Washington, *Bracebridge Hall*
(1822).

154

———, 'The Mutability of Literature', in *The Sketch Book of Geoffrey Crayon, Gent.* (rev. edn, 1848).

Jackson, Holbrook, 'G. K. Chesterton' (1908), in *Romance and Reality: Essays and Studies* (1911). Reproduced by permission of the Society of Authors as the Literary Representative of the Estate of Holbrook Jackson.

———, *The Anatomy of Bibliomania* (London, Faber and Faber, 1950). Reproduced by permission of the Society of Authors as the Literary Representative of the Estate of Holbrook Jackson.

Jacot de Boinod, Adam, 'Foreword', in *The Meaning of Tingo and Other Extraordinary Words from Around the World* (London, Penguin, 2005). Copyright © 2005 by Adam Jacot de Boinod. Reproduced by permission of the author, Penguin Books Ltd and The Penguin Press, a division of Penguin Group (USA) Inc.

Johnson, Dr Samuel, *Dictionary of the English Language* (1755).

———, *Preface to Shakespeare* (1765).

———, 'Rochester', 'Swift', 'Pope', in *Lives of the Poets*, vol. I (1779), vol. II (1780), vol. III (1791).

Johnson, Willis Fletcher, 'My Books', in *Ballads of Books*, ed. James Branden Matthews (1887).

Keats, John, 'On First Looking into Chapman's Homer', *Examiner* (1 December 1816).

Kingsmill, Hugh, reviewing Hugh Kenner's *Paradox in Chesterton* in *New English Review Magazine* (1948); reprinted in *The Best of Hugh Kingsmill*, ed. Michael Holroyd (London, Gollancz, 1970). Reproduced by permission of the Reverend Brooke Kingsmill-Lunn.

Kops, Bernard, 'Whitechapel Library, Aldgate East', in *Grandchildren and Other Poems* (London, Hearing Eye, 2000). Reproduced by permission of the author.

Lahr, John, *Prick Up Your Ears: A Biography of Joe Orton* (London, Allen Lane, 1978; reprinted by Bloomsbury and the University of California Press, 2002). Copyright © John Lahr 1978. Reproduced by permission of John Lahr, Bloomsbury Books and the University of California Press.

Lamb, Charles, 'The Two Races of Man', in *Elia* (1823).

———, 'Detached Thoughts on Books and Reading', in *Last Essays of Elia* (1833).

Landor, Walter Savage, 'Southey and Landor: Second Conversation', in *Imaginary Conversations, Works* IV (1848).

Lang, Andrew, 'The Ballad of the Bookworm', in *Ballads of Books*, ed. James Branden Matthews (1887).

———, *The Library* (2nd edn, 1892).

——— (ed.), *Ballads of Books* (1888).

Lansky, Aaron, *Outwitting History: How a Young Man Rescued a Million Books and Saved a Vanishing Civilisation* (London, Souvenir, 2004). Reproduced by permission of Aaron Lansky and Algonquin Books of Chapel Hill.

Lawrence, D. H., 'Surgery for the Novel – or a Bomb', *International Book Review* (April 1923); reprinted in *Phoenix: The Posthumous Papers of D. H. Lawrence*, ed. Edward D. McDonald (1936).

———, *A Propos of Lady Chatterley's Lover* (1930).

———, letter to Lady Ottoline Morrell, 30 April 1915; to Aldous Huxley, 15 August 1928; to Morris Ernst, 10 November 1928, in *The Letters of David Herbert Lawrence*, ed. Aldous Huxley (1932).

Lewis, C. S., *Surprised By Joy: The Shape of My Early Life* (London, Geoffrey Bles, 1955). Copyright © C. S. Lewis Pte Ltd 1955 and renewed 1984 by Arthur Owen Barfield. Reproduced by permission of C. S. Lewis Pte Ltd and Harcourt, Inc.

Lewis, Matthew, *The Monk* (1796).

Macaulay, Thomas Babington, 'John Dryden', *Edinburgh Review* (January 1828); reprinted in *The Works of Lord Macaulay*, Vol. V: *Critical and Historical Essays*, ed. Lady Trevelyan (1826).

Mackail, Denis, *Greenery Street* (London, William Heinemann, 1925; reprinted by Persephone Books, 2002). Reproduced by permission of Persephone Books.

Mandelstam, Osip, 'The Bookcase', in *The Prose of Osip Mandelstam*, trans. Clarence Brown (Princeton, Princeton University Press, 1965); reprinted as *The Noise of Time: Selected Prose*, trans. Clarence Brown (Evanston, IL, Northwestern University Press, 2002). Reproduced by permission of Northwestern University Press.

Marks, Joseph, *Harrap's French–English Dictionary of Slang and Colloquialisms*, revised and completed by Georgette A. Marks and Albert J. Farmer (London, Chambers Harrap Publishers, 1970). Copyright © by Georgette Marks 1970. Reproduced by permission of Chambers Harrap Publishers Ltd.

Matthews, James Branden (ed.), *Ballads of Books* (1887).

Maugham, W. Somerset, 'The Book Bag' (Florence, 1932); reprinted in *Complete Short Stories* (London, William Heinemann, 1951; Vintage, 2000). Reproduced by permission of The Random House Group Ltd and Julian Hope, representing the Literary Estate of Somerset Maugham.

Mencken, H. L., *Minority Report: H. L. Mencken's Notebooks* (New York, Alfred A. Knopf, 1956). Reproduced by permission of the Enoch Pratt Free Library, Baltimore, in accordance with the terms of the bequest of H. L. Mencken.

———, *On Politics: A Carnival of Buncombe*, ed. Malcolm Moos (Baltimore, Johns Hopkins Press, 1956). Reproduced by permission of the Enoch Pratt Free Library, Baltimore, in accordance with the terms of the bequest of H. L. Mencken.

Meyer, David, *Memoirs of a Book Snake* (Glenwood, IL, Waltham Street Press, 2001). Reproduced by permission of Meyerbooks.

Meynell, Everard, *The Life of Francis Thompson* (1913).

Mill, John Stuart, 'On the Liberty of Thought and Discussion', in *On Liberty* (1859).

———, *Autobiography* (1873).

Milton, John, *Lycidas* (1637).

———, *Areopagitica: A Speech for the Liberty of UNLICENS'D PRINTING* (1644).

Montaigne, Michel de, 'Of Three Commerces', in *Essayes*, trans. John Florio (1613).

Moore, George, *Literature at Nurse or Circulating Morals* (1885).

Morley, Christopher, *The Haunted Bookshop* (1920; new edn, London, Faber and Faber, 1951).

Morris, William, 'A Note by William Morris on his Aims in Founding the Kelmscott Press' (1891).

Murray, Sir James A. H., *The Evolution of English Lexicography* (Romanes Lecture, 1900).

————, letter to Lord Bryce, 15 December 1903, quoted in K. M. Elisabeth Murray, *Caught in the Web of Words: James A. H. Murray and the Oxford English Dictionary* (London, Yale University Press, 1977). Reproduced by permission of B. N. Murray.

Nabokov, Vladimir, 'Good Readers and Good Writers', introductory essay to *Lectures on Literature*, ed. Fredson Bowers (London, Weidenfeld & Nicolson, 1980). By arrangement with the Estate of Vladimir Nabokov; all rights reserved.

Newton, Edward, *Amenities of Book-Collecting and Kindred Affections* (1920).

Norwich, John Julius, *Christmas Crackers, 1970–1979: Being Ten Commonplace Selections* (London, Allen Lane, 1980).

————, *Still More Christmas Crackers, 1990–1999: Being Ten Commonplace Selections* (London, Viking, 2000).

O'Brien, Flann (Patrick Nolan), from one of his 'Cruiskeen Lawn' columns in the *Irish Times*; reprinted in *The Best of Myles* (London, MacGibbon & Kee, 1968). Copyright © The Estate of the Late Brian O'Nolan. Reproduced by permission of A M Heath & Company Ltd on behalf of the Estate.

Orton, Joe, *Loot* (Methuen, 1967); reprinted in *The Complete Plays of Joe Orton* (Eyre Methuen, 1976; Grove Press, 1977). Reproduced by permission of Methuen Drama, an imprint of A & C Black Ltd.

Orwell, George, 'Literature and Totalitarianism' (broadcast, 1941). Copyright © George Orwell, 1936 and 1941. Reproduced by permission of Bill Hamilton as the Literary Executor of the Estate of the Late Sonia Brownell Orwell, Secker

& Warburg Ltd and Harcourt, Inc.

————, 'Bookshop Memories' (1936), in *The Collected Essays, Journalism and Letters of George Orwell, Volume 1: An Age Like This*, ed. Sonia Orwell and Ian Angus (London, Secker & Warburg, 1968). Copyright © George Orwell, 1936 and 1941. Reproduced by permission of Bill Hamilton as the Literary Executor of the Estate of the Late Sonia Brownell Orwell, Secker & Warburg Ltd and Harcourt, Inc.

Ovid, *Amores*, ii.10, trans. Christopher Marlowe (*c*.1600).

Palladas, *Greek Anthology*, xi.381, in Robin Skelton, *Two Hundred Poems from the Greek Anthology* (London, Methuen, 1971).

Parker, Dorothy, *New Yorker* (5 November 1927).

Peacock, Thomas Love, *Nightmare Abbey* (1818).

Peck, Samuel Minturn, 'Among my Books' (1886), in James Branden Matthews (ed.), *Ballads of Books* (1887).

Pennac, Daniel, *Comme un roman* (Paris, Éditions Gallimard, 1992), trans. Matthew J. Reisz; published in English as *Reads like a Novel*, trans. Daniel Gunn (London, Quartet Books, 1994). Copyright © Éditions Gallimard, 1992. Reproduced by permission of Éditions Gallimard.

Poe, Edgar Allan, 'The Philosophy of Composition', *Graham's Magazine* (April 1846).

Pope, Alexander, *An Essay on Criticism* (1711).

————, Preface to his translation of the *Iliad* (1715).

————, 'Epistle IV to Richard Boyle, Earl of Burlington: Of the Use of RICHES' (1731).

————, *Dunciad*, bk IV (1743).

———— (pseud. Esdras Barnivelt, Apothecary), *A Key to the Lock* (1715).

Pound, Ezra, *How to Read* (London, Desmond Harmsworth, 1931); reproduced in *The Literary Essays of Ezra Pound*, edited with an Introduction by T. S. Eliot (London, Faber and Faber, 1954). Copyright © 1935 by Ezra Pound. Reproduced by permission of New Directions Publishing Corp. and Faber and Faber Ltd.

Powell, Lawrence Clark, *Books in My Baggage: Adventures in Reading and Collecting* (London, Constable, 1960). Reproduced by permission of the L. C. Powell Estate.

Price, Rev. Edward D., and W. G. Hartog (eds), *British Universities Modern English Illustrated Dictionary* (1924).

Raabe, Tom, *Biblioholism: The Literary Addiction* (Golden, CO, Fulcrum Publishing, 1991). Copyright © 2001 Fulcrum Publishing, Inc., Golden, Colorado. Reproduced by permission; all rights reserved.

Rejwan, Nissim, *The Last Jews in Baghdad: Remembering a Lost Homeland* (Austin, Tex., University of Texas Press, 2004). Reproduced by permission of the University of Texas Press.

Richards, I. A., 'Toward a Theory of Translating', in *Studies in Chinese Thought*, ed. Arthur F. Wright (Chicago, University of Chicago Press, 1953). Reproduced by permission of the Literary Estate of I. A. and D. E. Richards.

Rosten, Leo Calvin, *The New Joys of Yiddish*, ed. Lawrence Bush (London, Arrow Books, 2003). Copyright © 2001 by the Rosten Family LLC. Reproduced by permission of the Rosten Family

LLC and the Random House Group Ltd.

Ruskin, John, *Sesame and Lilies* (1865).

Russell, Bertrand, letter to R. W. Clark, July 1965, in Nicholas Griffin (ed.), *The Selected Letters of Bertrand Russell: The Public Years, 1914–1970* (London, Routledge, 2001). Reproduced by permission of the Bertrand Russell Peace Foundation Ltd.

'S., W.', *Spectator* (10 December 1881).

Saxe, John Godfrey, 'The Library', in *Ballads of Books*, ed. James Branden Matthews (1887).

Seth, Vikram, *Two Lives* (London, Little, Brown, 2005; New York, HarperCollins, 2005). Copyright © by Vikram Seth. Reproduced by permission of Harper-Collins Publishers and Little, Brown Book Group.

Shakespeare, William, *Love's Labour's Lost*, IV.2 (*c.*1597).

Shandler, Jeffrey (ed.), *Awakening Lives: Autobiographies of Jewish Youth in Poland before the Holocaust* (Yale University Press in co-operation with YIVO, 2002). Copyright © 2002 by The YIVO Institute for Jewish Research. Reproduced by permission of Yale University Press.

Shaw, George Bernard, Preface to *The Shewing-up of Blanco Posnet*, in *The Doctor's Dilemma, Getting Married & The Shewing-up of Blanco Posnet* (London, Constable, 1911). Reproduced by permission of the Society of Authors, on behalf of the Bernard Shaw Estate.

Shelley, P. B., *Adonais*, XL (1821).

Sheridan, Richard Brinsley, *The Rivals* (1775).

Sheridan, Dr Thomas, 'A Letter to the Dean [Jonathan Swift] When in England' (1726), reprinted in *The Poems of Jonathan Swift*, ed. William Ernst Browning, vol. II (1910).

Sherman, Frank Dempster, 'The Book-Hunter' (1885), in *Ballads of Books*, ed. James Branden Matthews (1887).

Shorter Oxford English Dictionary, ed. William Trumble and Lesley Brown (Oxford, Oxford University Press, 5th edn 2002). Reproduced by permission of Oxford University Press.

Skelton, Robin, *Two Hundred Poems from the Greek Anthology* (London, Methuen, 1971). Reproduced by courtesy of A. and B. Skelton.

Smart, Christopher, 'Jubilate Agno Fragment B1', MS (1758–63).

Smith, Logan Pearsall, *Afterthoughts* (1931).

Smith, Miles, 'Translators to the Reader', Introduction to Miles Smith and Thomas Bilson (eds), *The Authorised Version of the Bible* (1611); quoted (modernised) in Alister McGrath, *In the Beginning: The Story of the King James Bible and How It Changed a Nation, a Language and a Culture* (London, Hodder & Stoughton, 2001).

Smith, Sydney, in *A Memoir of the Reverend Sydney Smith by his Daughter Lady Holland* (1855).

Snelling, O. F., *Rare Books and Rarer People: Some Personal Reminiscences of 'The Trade'* (London, Werner Shaw, 1982). Reproduced by permission of Barry Shaw of Werner Shaw Ltd.

Stark, Freya, *Traveller's Prelude: Autobiography 1853–1927* (London, John Murray, 1950; reprinted by Century Classics, 1983). Reproduced by kind permission of John R. Murray.

Stephen, Leslie, 'Some Words about Sir Walter Scott', in *Hours in a Library*, vol. I (1874).

Stevenson, Robert Louis, *The Ebb-Tide* (1894).

———, 'Picture-books in Winter', in *A Child's Garden of Verses* (1885).

Strachey, Lytton, 'The Lives of the Poets' (1906), 'Madame du Deffand' (1913), 'Henri Beyle' (1914), in *Books and Characters* (1922).

Struther, Jan, *Mrs Miniver* (Chatto & Windus, 1939). Reproduced by permission of Little, Brown Book Group and Harcourt, Inc.

Swift, Jonathan, *A Tale of a Tub* (1704).

Tennyson, Lord, in Hallam Tennyson, *Alfred Lord Tennyson: A Memoir by His Son* (1897).

Thackeray, William Makepeace, *The History of Pendennis* (1848–50).

———, 'Sorrows of Werther', in *Ballads* (1855).

Thomas, Edward, 'Digressions on Fish and Fishing', 'Recollections of November', in *Horae Solitariae* (1902).

Thoreau, Henry David, 'Reading', in *Walden* (1854).

Tomlinson, Henry Major, *Out of Soundings* (1931).

Trench, Richard Chenevix, *On Some Deficiencies in Our English Dictionaries* (1857).

Trollope, Anthony, *An Autobiography* (1883).

Twain, Mark, 'Fenimore Cooper's Literary Offences', in *How to Tell a Story and Other Essays* (1897).

Tyas, Shaun (ed.), *Book-worm Droppings: An Anthology of Absurd Remarks Made by Customers in Secondhand Bookshops* (Stamford, Paul Watkins, 1988). Reproduced by permission of Shaun Tyas.

Tyndale, William, *The Obedience of a*

Christian Man (1528; modernised Penguin edn, 2000).

Vaughan, Henry, 'To His Books', 'On Thomas Bodley's Library', in *Thalia Dediviva* (1678).

Vincent, David, *Bread, Knowledge and Freedom: A Study of Nineteenth-Century Working-Class Autobiography* (London, Europa Publications, 1981).

Virgil, 'The Tenth Pastoral', trans. John Dryden (1697).

Walton, Izaak, *The Life of Mr. George Herbert* (1670).

Waugh, Evelyn, *A Handful of Dust* (London, Chapman & Hall, 1934). Copyright © 1934 by Evelyn Waugh; renewed copyright © 1962 by Evelyn Waugh. Reproduced by permission of Penguin Books Ltd and Little, Brown and Co., Inc.

Webster, Noah, *Dissertations on the English Language* (1789).

Wells, John, *Rude Words: A Discursive History of the London Library* (London, Macmillan, 1991). Copyright © John Wells. Reproduced by permission of the Estate of John Wells c/o Rogers, Coleridge & White Ltd.

Wesley, Charles, *The Journal of the Rev. Charles Wesley* (1774).

Whitlock, Richard, *Zootomia* (1654).

Wilson, Frances, *Literary Seductions: Compulsive Writers and Diverted Readers* (London, Faber and Faber, 1999). Reproduced by permission of Faber and Faber Ltd.

Wirsén, K. D. af, 'Love and Books', trans. from the Swedish by Edmund Gosse, in *Ballads of Books*, ed. Andrew Lang (1888).

Wood, Thomas, *The Autobiography of Thomas Wood, 1822–1880* (1956),

quoted in David Vincent, *Bread, Knowledge and Freedom: A Study of Nineteenth-Century Working-Class Autobiography* (London, Europa Publications, 1981).

Woolf, Leonard, *Beginning Again: An Autobiography of the Years 1911–1918* (London, Hogarth Press, 1964). Reproduced by permission of the University of Sussex and the Society of Authors as their representative.

Woolf, Virginia, 'How Should One Read a Book?', *Yale Review* (October 1926); reprinted in *The Common Reader Second Series* (London, Hogarth Press, 1932). Copyright © 1932 by Harcourt, Inc.; renewed © 1960 by Leonard Woolf. Reproduced by permission of the Society of Authors as the Literary Representative of the Estate of Virginia Woolf and Harcourt, Inc.

———, 'Reviewing' (1939); reprinted in *The Captain's Death Bed and Other Essays* (London, Hogarth Press, 1950). Copyright © 1950 and renewed 1978 by Harcourt, Inc. Reproduced by permission of the Society of Authors as the Literary Representative of the Estate of Virginia Woolf, and Harcourt, Inc.

Wordsworth, William, 'Poems Dedicated to National Independence and Liberty', *Morning Post*, no. xvi (16 April 1803).

———, *The Prelude* (1850).

Yevtushenko, Yevgeny, *A Precocious Autobiography*, trans. Andrew R. MacAndrew (London, Collins & Harvill Press, 1963; New York, Dutton, 1963). Copyright © 1963 by E. P. Dutton, renewed © 1991 by Penguin USA. Copyright © 1963, renewed © 1991 by Yevgeny Yevtushenko. Reproduced by permission of Dutton, a division of Penguin Group (USA) Inc.